1st ptd Aug 1932, this
is a Sept 1932 second.
gives names, amounts,
dates, + purposes of spending of
a great deal of money for
largely political favors / pork
barrell, + favoritism .

3280101034

2x-3

WASHINGTON SWINDLE SHEET

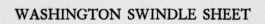

WASHINGTON SWINDLE SHEET

By
WILLIAM P. HELM

ALBERT & CHARLES BONI
NEW YORK   MCMXXXII

Printed in the United States of America

CONTENTS

5

PREFACE

For the better part of the last seventeen years, the author has been a newspaper correspondent at Washington. He is, perhaps, the only correspondent at the capital who has not a speaking acquaintance with a single member of Congress.

Such a position is unique. It follows that the story presented here is impersonal. It is purely a reporter's story. It favors with the bias of personal friendship none of the characters that appear in its pages, and, let us hope, it does none of them a wrong. The intent has been simply to follow the record as it lies, to record its salient facts and to interpret them.

It has seemed to the author that those facts might be of value to the American people at a time when they are about to select their various spokesmen in House and Senate. If this volume has such value, it will have met the purpose for which it was designed.

Washington, D. C.
July 6, 1932.

WASHINGTON SWINDLE SHEET

Chapter I

"Easy Come, Easy Go"

In bookkeeper's slang, the expense account is known as the swindle sheet. That meaning is in mind in choosing the title for this book. For this is a tale of the world's greatest swindle sheet—the expense account of the Senate of the United States. A single year, 1931, has been selected.

There are ninety-six men in the United States Senate. They fix their own spendings. No officious auditor may blue-pencil the items they put down on the swindle sheet. Many Senators spend public money they would not dream of spending from their own pockets. At Washington and on vacation they coddle their personal whims and foibles at public expense. Their motto is "Easy come, easy go." Open-handed and big-hearted, they lavish the treasury substance from one end of America to the other.

In fact, every Senator starts his public career by perpetrating a petty swindle upon the people of the United States. The cheating begins when he hurries for his train to Washington. The swindle operates even before he takes the oath of office. It consists of his taking from the treasury, to cover his trip, a sum approximately four

11

times as much as his actual, necessary traveling expenses. He calls it mileage; but the public has another name for it—graft. If it is graft, it is legalized graft; Senators have been doing it since their grandpas wore diapers.

That particular graft has been legalized for two generations; others are of later coinage. A Senator from a distant State thus can slip a thousand dollars into his pocketbook every year—a thousand dollars for which the public receives no return whatever. Five hundred dollars of that sort of graft is only fair-to-middling pickings. Sorry, indeed, is the homesite of a Senator who is unable to make a profit of at least two hundred dollars a year in mileage. A generous Senate has made this graft respectable; a thrifty Senate pockets it.

At the Capitol, the arriving Senator lunches or dines in a private restaurant staffed by 80-odd waiters and cooks, all on the public pay roll. Roman baths, where Senatorial torsoes alone may lave, are next on the listing of his perquisites. A barber shop where the government buys him a shaving mug for a dollar and a half and puts thereon his name in gilded letters (cost, six bits), likewise awaits his Solonic pleasure. There he may be perfumed, shaved, tonicked, singed, shined and hair-cutted for a "thank you." Even that pay is not really necessary; the taxpayers maintain the establishment.

He sits in quarters air-cooled and air-conditioned. He drinks his choice of half a dozen kinds of spring water, bottled and brought to him at the trifling public cost of

five cents a tumbler. If he prefers, he may have apollinaris water instead. The taxpayers buy it for him by the
case in those nice little bottles known as splits. Or if Nature dawdles, our Senator may quaff Pluto water. It is
bought for him, by the case, at public expense.

Of clerk hire, he provides himself with abundance, and
no man is there to say No if he wishes to put his brother,
his son, his nephew, his niece or any other family scion
on the public roll. When he writes a letter it is sent
through the mails free of cost—to him. When he makes
a speech, there is a force of bright young people to fold
the document as it comes from the government print-
shop, insert it in a franked envelope and send it on its
way to whomever he wishes to propagandize. The folding, the postage are paid for out of the treasury.

On vacation, he may hie himself to the mountains in
summer and the Sunny South in winter, likewise at public
expense. He may take cross-country airplane flights, or
fish where dancing waters trill at the base of snow-capped
mountains, or laze away the hours in picnic lunches in the
Far West. The public treasury will pay his carfare,
buy his bait, and furnish his lunch. Also, the public
treasury will pay his hotel bills, tip the bellboys who leap
to obey him, press his pants and cross the palm of his
valet not with silver, but with crisp currency.

Does he wish to pose as Lord Bountiful, the generous
representative of a rich and powerful nation? Then he
may stand treat to ten or twenty, or as many more as

lie within his vision; the taxpayers will foot the bill. Now he is found tipping steamboat captains and stewards, chambermaids, horse wranglers, waitresses, housekeepers, utility boys, stenographers and chefs with sums that range from silver coins to double eagles—all from the public purse.

Does Washington pall during the lull of the Christmas holidays? Then he may swing down to Florida, charter a houseboat or two, go aloft in an airplane or a blimp, and feast and strut in the mellow sunshine without thought of wintry blasts chilling the bread-lines to the North. The government pays his fare, his subsistence, his houseboat hire and all the rest.

Why? The government pays all these charges and many others because the Senate, having no supervision of its expenses other than its own supervision, says that the government must pay them. By the government is meant the taxpayers. You and You and You and all of us, smiling happily now under a fresh levy of a billion dollars a year. A part of that billion will be ladled out this year to give our noble Senators the things craved by their sensitive souls. The public puts the money into the treasury and the Senate takes it out. It's quite simple.

Once every year the Secretary of the Senate makes a public accounting of these spendings. All that have been mentioned thus far and many others that will follow are taken from the Secretary's accounting. They are contained in his annual Report for 1931, the fiscal year beginning July 1, 1930, and ending June 30, 1931. The Report is printed as Senate Document No. 1. The record thus is at once accurate and official. It is all there, in the Secretary's Annual Report, for the inspection of anyone who wishes to see it.

From that Report this book, in the main, is written. Not an entry is recorded here that is not recorded there, or in other official documents. This tale, therefore, is a true tale of the national swindle sheet. If not, the error lies in the documents from which it is compiled.

Chapter II

On to Washington—at Forty Cents a Mile!

It was a turbulent session. All through the month of June, Congress, peevish and disheartened, had sweltered under the Capitol dome. A third of the Senators and all the Representatives, facing the election campaign of 1930, were clamoring for adjournment. Back home fences in sad disrepair were held by subordinates who wired frantically to Washington imploring relief. And still the interminable session dragged on.

Finally, on the eve of Independence Day, to the intense relief not only of the lawmakers but of almost everybody else in the United States, Congress adjourned.

Immediately thereupon President Hoover called the Senate in extraordinary session to ratify the London treaty on limitation of naval armaments. The dismay of some of the Senators, badly needed in the reelection campaigns at home, was profound. On second thought their feeling was tempered: Mr. Hoover had designated July 7—only four days thence—as the opening day; the session promised to be short; there yet might be time to ratify the treaty and get away from Washington before the elections were lost.

16

So the House, whose services were not necessary in treaty-making, went home while the Senate prepared to make the best of it. And Old Man Mileage licked his chops. The smell of gravy was in the air.

On the morning of the 7th, Senator Phillips Lee Goldsborough of Maryland left his Baltimore home to attend the session. From Baltimore to Washington is a forty minute train-ride. The railroad fare is $1.44. A seat in the parlor car is 75 cents more, bringing the total one-way cost to $2.19. Allowing as much more to take Senator Goldsborough home at the close of the session, his necessary traveling expenses amounted to $4.38.

To cover this $4.38 expense, Senator Goldsborough received $16 from the United States treasury. The difference between the $4.38 necessary expense and the $16 he received is $11.62. That small sum represents the personal profit made possible to the Senator on the trip. Did he take the $16? Of course he did! Openly, legally and in accord with custom going back to 1866 when Congress established a rate of 40 cents a mile to cover the traveling expenses of a Senator or Representative to Washington to attend a session.

In collecting his mileage and his profit—$11.62 for riding 80 minutes in a pullman car—Senator Goldsborough was in distinguished company. All his colleagues attending the session lined up at the disbursing officer's desk. All made money on their mileage. Mr.

Goldsborough, living nearer to Washington than the others, stood to make the least.

Some Senators, the record shows, made tidy profits. Senator Black of Alabama, for instance. He drew $305.20. The railroad fare from Birmingham, his home, to Washington and return, plus the two-way cost of a lower pullman berth, is $72.10. Mr. Black in a lower berth stood to make a profit of $233.10, excluding meals and tips en route. His necessary traveling expenses were somewhat less than one-fourth of what he drew from the treasury to cover them.

Senator Wagner of New York drew $96. If he took the night train to Washington, his fare and a lower berth cost $11.89. Returning in the same manner—the cost for a lower berth being more than of a seat in a parlor car, which he could have taken had the five-hour trip been made by daylight—his fare home cost $11.89 more; that made $23.78 for the round trip. The difference between the $96 he drew from the treasury and $23.78, the actual fare, is $72.22. That trifling sum was available as his personal profit. It averages somewhat more than seven dollars an hour of actual riding time.

LaFollette, the insurgent, coming on from Madison, Wisconsin, could have purchased railroad and lower-berth pullman tickets both ways for $82.92. He drew $371.60 from the treasury. Thus $288.68 was available for the LaFollette private pocketbook.

Borah of Idaho, hailing from the Far West, drew

$1,058.80 to cover his mileage. The necessary railroad fare, both ways, was $239.56. Senator Borah's excess, therefore, amounted to $819.24. It was Senator Borah who later protested that this graft was unfair to the tax-payers. Appearing before a congressional committee he suggested that the committee eliminate the excess. The committee, however, itself enjoying the time-honored custom, took no action on the Senator's request.

Capper, friend of the farmer, coming on from the land of 10-cent eggs, 30-cent wheat and 5-cent beef cattle, drew his forty cents a mile on more than 1,200 miles (the length of a one-way trip), although his necessary railroad and pullman fare amounted to but $114.68 for the round trip. What he drew was $494.40; what he needed to spend was $114.68; what was left, $379.72, would have sufficed to buy enough eggs, wheat and beef to last the Senator through many a lean month. He could have spent it that way had he wanted to; the $379.72 was available, in all legality, for his own private purse.

Fess of Ohio, darling of the prohibitionists and other moralists, drew $249.20 mileage to cover a round trip whose railroad and pullman fare totaled only $50.78. The excess of $198.42, representing legalized graft permitted under the custom, was available for his private pocket or for any other purpose to which he wished to apply it.

Harrison of Mississippi, silver-tongued champion of the downtrodden, snagged $430 in mileage to cover a trip where the railroad and lower berth charges, both ways, amounted to only $99.16. What Senator Harrison did with the other $330.84 for which the public got no return is known only to himself.

Reed Smoot of Utah heads the Senate finance committee. As chairman of that committee he helped to fashion the new billion-dollar tax bill. Senator Smoot put $978 of public funds into his pocket to cover a round trip from Provo, Utah, to Washington that any other man, woman or child can make for $212.96, plus meals. The difference between what went into the Smoot pocket and what had to come out to meet essential railroad and pullman fare is $765.04. Such was the measure of personal profit possible to the Senator to help sustain him as he worked to place another billion-dollar tax levy on the public.

Walsh of Montana, guiding genius of the Teapot Dome revelations, for which Albert Fall was sent to the penitentiary, drew $951.20 in mileage. Railroad and pullman transportation from Helena, Montana, where Senator Walsh lives, to Washington and return costs $210.72. The difference between what Senator Walsh got and what he had to pay out is $740.48. For information as to what was done with that $740.48, inquire of Thomas J. Walsh, Senate Office Building, Washington, D. C.

Jones of Washington, author of that pleasant bit of legislation under which prohibition law violators may be sentenced to from five to ten years in the penitentiary, pocketed $1,074.22 over and above necessary traveling expenses. Senator Jones drew $1,347.20 in mileage. The price-tag on railroad and pullman fares for the round trip reads $272.98. The difference went into the Jones pocketbook without violating any statute, five-and-ten or otherwise. What return did the public get for the $1,-074.22?

Bingham of Connecticut, distant from Washington but a short night's ride (New Haven), pocketed $122 to cover traveling expenses which to you, sir, would cost only $32.30. The difference of $89.70 represents personal profit working while he slept, at the rate of about seven dollars an hour.

Copeland of New York whose reputed income as a newspaper syndicate writer and broadcaster is many times his $10,000 salary as Senator accepted $94 of the tax-payers' money to make the round trip from Suffern, N. Y. Railroad and pullman fare for the round trip can be bought by anybody for $26.08. Dr. Copeland is not required to tell the public what happened to the other $67.92.

Multi-millionaire Couzens of Michigan, coming over from Detroit, needed to spend but $55.86 to cover fare and pullman charge. He drew $244 from the government, an excess of $188.14.

Hiram Johnson of California, whose public career is a monument against graft and corruption in politics, received from the Senate disbursing officer $1,292.80 in mileage. Thousands of his countrymen unknown to fame make the same trip—San Francisco to Washington and

21

return—at a cost of $274.76 for railroad and pullman fare. The difference, available for the Senator's private purse, is $1,018.04, less meals and tips en route.

Smith Wildman Brookhart, sharpshooter and Wall Street baiter, offered no objection when the government put into his pocket $416 to cover his round-trip fare and pullman charges from Washington, Iowa, to Washington, D. C. The railroad's published rates show that the actual cost of the trip, including lower pullman berth, is $96.54. Senator Brookhart's honorarium, in excess of necessary fare, was $319.46.

Wheeler of Montana, ardent Left-Winger of Democracy and vocal champion of the lowly, pocketed $946 as mileage for the round trip from his home in Butte to Washington. Any Butte miner can buy exactly the same service and accommodations for $210.72, considerably less than one-fourth of Senator Wheeler's mileage. The difference, $735.28, would hire that miner, at $4 a day, for six months.

Watson of Indiana, majority leader in the Senate, lives in the town of Rushville. Walk into the depot and price tickets to Washington; the station agent will tell you that the fare and lower berth both ways total $58.52. Senator Watson drew $255.20 in mileage, a trifle of $196.68 in excess of the actual fare.

Sheppard of Texas who played an unforgettable rôle in putting prohibition into the Constitution and is highly regarded by his colleagues in the Senate for his sterling qualities and integrity, received $483.60 to cover mileage from his home in Texarkana and return. Railroad and pullman fare can be bought over the counter for $116.76. The difference is $366.84.

The recital palls. The record for every Senator, in detail, is shown in Appendix A to this volume. Every member of the august Senate without exception found thus far dips into the public purse, year after year, and withdraws his hand with about four times as many dollars sticking to it as are really needed to transport him in comfort from his home to Washington and back.

Every Representative, too. There are 435 of them. Every mother's son of the lot—96 Senators, 435 Representatives, a total of 531—has Old Man Mileage working to enrich his private purse. Every year. Twice a year in years when there are extra sessions. Representatives receive the same modest sums as Senators, or 40 cents a mile all the way from home to Washington. And the taxpayers pay it. Is it to be wondered, then, that Mr. Taxpayer is universally cartooned as a cock-eyed boob?

A river of gravy, Old Man Mileage just keeps rolling along. It has become an old congressional custom, so why bring it up now? Hasn't it been done for more than sixty years? Wasn't it good enough for our fathers? Why, then, shouldn't it be good enough for us?

One of the delightful things about mileage is that the Senator or Representative drawing it need not have incurred the expense at all. It is assumed that he started for Washington from his home. Whether he actually starts from his home is of no interest to anyone. A Senator from the Far West, for instance, might visit friends in Alexandria, just across the Potomac, between sessions and take a bus or taxi over to the Capitol on the opening day. He would draw mileage from his home in the West just the same.

There is no meddling supervisor to say, "No, Senator; you hail not from the Rockies, but from Alexandria; nine miles for you and not three thousand." That particular Senator is presumed—by Senatorial courtesy or something—to have started from his home, three thousand miles away. He gets forty cents a mile for three thousand miles. Where he actually started from is irrelevant.

This custom brings one to a somewhat closer examination of the circumstances under which the Secretary of the Senate paid out more than $30,000 in mileage in July, 1930.

There was an interval of only four days between the ending of the regular session and the beginning of the special session. Did the Senators all go home in that brief interval and then turn around and start back for Washington? Does anyone believe that Senators living in distant States made such pointless and foolish trips? It was easy enough for Senators living nearby to spend the intervening time with the folks back home. The New England Senators could have done so, as could those

24

from the South and the Middle West. But what about the Senators living West of the Mississippi?

Unless they went home by airplane, the feat was impossible for most of them. Even then, the flying Senators would have had to turn around immediately and fly back to Washington. A few may have done this, but the majority doubtless remained in or near Washington. So it develops that in many cases the mileage paid individual Senators was all pure excess, less the cost of maintaining themselves for four days. They incurred no traveling expense, yet they took the mileage.

Thus some Senators undoubtedly accepted mileage at four times actual travel expense to cover a trip they did not take. Under law and custom, they were wholly within their rights. They took the money and put it in their pockets without giving the taxpayers the sorry return of one-fourth of their money's worth. They did not spend in traveling the usual 25 cents on each dollar they received; they spent nothing whatever, except sufficient to cover their living expenses in Washington or at nearby excursion points. That such grafting is regarded as entirely proper is shown by the fact that every Senator attending the special session took his mileage. The record discloses not a single exception.

The present mileage is defended by some persons on the grounds that a Senator receives mileage but once a year (when he comes to Washington to attend a session of Congress) and that in reality he travels a good deal between sessions at his own expense. This claim is not substantiated by the facts, as many Senators travel *at public expense* while Congress is not in session. Even if it were true, the transaction should be clean-cut; Senators should be paid for such traveling directly and not in a blanket mileage account.

As it stands now, congressional mileage is tainted. It would be easy to remove the taint and provide adequate— but not extravagant—mileage for necessary public traveling between sessions. No fair-minded person could object to that, but every man or woman with a sense of fair play feels outraged by the present custom.

Congress appropriates every year $51,000 for mileage for the Senate and $175,000 for mileage for the House, a total of $226,000. That covers attendance at the regular session of Congress each year; when a special or extra session is held another appropriation of approximately the same amount is made.

Three-fourths of the $226,000 now appropriated is graft, no more or less, in that mileage paid individuals averages more than four times as much as necessary railroad and pullman fare. Here the taxpayers are mulcted approximately $170,000 for the private pocketbooks of those entrusted with the public welfare. This dribble of waste from the treasury has been dribbling since 1866, when the law was passed.

If Congress were to cut its present mileage appropriation squarely in two, there still would be left sufficient to permit every Senator and Representative to travel from his home to Washington and return, bringing his wife with him and occupying a pullman drawing room both ways. One-half of the present appropriation, or $113,000 a year, would cover the entire expense including meals and tips. Such an appropriation would mean an average of $213 a year for every member of Congress.

Chapter III

Vacation, and Wild Life

Vacation days crept to their rendezvous on the calendar in mid-July, 1930. The seven-month regular session and the brief extra session ended; the heat beat down mercilessly on the sticky asphalt of Washington's broad streets; the mountains and the Northland beckoned with windswept fingers; and the Senate of the United States scattered to the four points of the compass.

Now, there are wise men in the United States Senate, wise in the ways of their fathers, and wise in their own natural wisdom. A part of that wisdom, garnered through years of service in the Upper Chamber, covers the art of taking a vacation. Different is the senatorial art from the layman's; for while the vacation-bound private citizen looks first to his purse and pays his way accordingly, the vacationing Senator need do neither.

If he is fore-fending—as many of our ablest senatorial minds are—he looks first to his vacation along in March or April. He then anticipates the dog-days by resolution or committee task. In other words, he gives himself a vacation job before the session ends. Thus armed, the United States treasury pays his way and he may appoint

28

his conscience as his guide in planning what he will spend and where he will go.

On April 17, 1930, three months before the special session ended, the Senate adopted a resolution under which a committee, headed by Senator Walcott of Connecticut, was authorized to investigate the wild animal life of the country and to recommend new laws to conserve it.

Not long thereafter the committee began to function. One of its first acts was to employ a secretary, Morris Legendre, at $5,000 a year, and a special investigator, Carl Shoemaker, at $4,500. In time two clerks were added to the force. Office furniture was purchased and a press-clipping bureau was employed. The actual investigation appears to have got under way early in the following fiscal year with the dispatch of Mr. Shoemaker (on July 4) on a trip from Washington to Portland, Oregon, and return.

That was the beginning of a long and wonderful party; of junkets to the mountains, of lazing down broad rivers, of cross-country airplane flights, and of sitting at pullman windows and watching the wild life flit past; of picnic lunches and fishing trips; of free spendings and lavish tips scattered over most of the United States. In a word, it was the start of a trip on the fat of the land.

The time all this happened was but yesterday—the summer and fall of 1930 and the winter and spring of 1931. It was a time, fresh memory recalls, of national distress and privation; a time when ragged and hungry

29

millions vainly sought employment; when women and children, ill-nourished and worse clad, cried for food and shelter; when there was at least one bread-line in every city of the land and when those who begged food in the winding lines were numbered by the hundreds of thousands. That was the time.

The long party with its gay and care-free flittings cost approximately $27,000. Seven names appear as spenders in the various expense accounts cashed by the treasury. The first is Morris Legendre, the secretary of the committee, who cleared most of the spendings. Next is his confrere, Mr. Shoemaker. The others are Senators Walcott, the chairman; Hawes of Missouri; Pittman of Nevada; Norbeck of South Dakota, and McNary of Oregon.

McNary's name appears only once, when he received a lump sum of $500 for which he accounted with a blanket expense account naming only "actual expenses" while engaged on the committee's assignment.

Although the committee started in to investigate wild life early in July, its bills did not begin to pour in to the cashier until mid-November. The committee apparently was too busy to make out expense accounts. But when the bills did come in, they came in a torrent. The first of those November bills amounted to $4,568.18. In two days, they ran to a total of $9,124.14, including Mr. Legendre's salary for three months. The two-day bills

30

covered most of the expenses of the committee for four months.

One of the first bills was for a junket to Toronto. There were four men in that party—Senators Walcott and Hawes and Messrs. Legendre and Shoemaker. The trip was made in the torrid season, when the country sweltered under an August sun. Walcott, Hawes, Shoemaker and Legendre decided to investigate wild life at the Royal York Hotel, Toronto. Thither they journeyed to attend a convention of the International Association of Fish and Game Commissioners.

There the quartet with the United States treasury to draw on stood magnificent treat. The bills show their food and lodging cost the American taxpayers $265.57 for two days, August 25 and 26. The food is not itemized in the expense accounts, so it is impossible to say what they ate and drank. Who ate and drank with them are not identified, save that their guests were other "conservationists." How and where they ate and drank likewise are not disclosed. Apparently, a great deal of it went on. One can only imagine the scene, set, let us say, in a great dining room with many present and participating.

"Hey, Commish, fill her up again with this delicious venison steak! Make mine codfish balls with a chaser of Little Necks! Here's looking at you, Warden; join me in this prime New York beef! A pony of Rocky Fords for mine, please! No, no—really, I've had all I care for; but, if you insist, I'll take a tomato surprise! Say when, old man, on this Long Island duckling! A schooner of vegetable soup, please!"

Some such jargon, possibly, enlivened the gay party. On these tantalizing details, however, Legendre's expense account is mute. Here's all it says:

> Royal York Hotel bill for party (Senator Walcott, Senator Hawes, Mr. Shoemaker, and secretary) including luncheons and dinners given to conservationists present at convention, $265.57.

The money thus spent for food during those two days at Toronto was sufficient to pay the grocery bills of the average American family four months. What of it? Nothing, of course. Nothing at all. The next entry in the expense account shows that even this average spending of $34 a day per man failed to appease the senatorial appetite:

> Additional bill of Royal York Hotel mailed to Washington for restaurant service the night the party left Toronto, $13.55.

A mere trifle, that item. Other mere trifles spent investigating wild life at the Royal York Hotel include the following items gleaned from the Legendre expense account rendered the Senate pay-off man:

32

August 24.

Tips to porters, at lunch and service during day, $6.00.

Cigars, cigarettes, mineral waters, etc., necessary for committee's entertainment, $6.00.

August 25.

Tips to waiters for breakfast, lunch, dinner and for other service during the day, $12.00.

August 26.

Tips to waiters and maître d'hôtel, $10.00.

Tips to porters carrying luggage for entire party from hotel to train, $4.00.

Tips to valet service at hotel for party, $5.00.

Tips for room service at hotel for entire party, $5.00.

Forty-six dollars thus were paid out in tips in three days, not including tips paid train porters and others. The total cost to the taxpayers of this little dash of Messrs. Walcott, Hawes, Legendre and Shoemaker into Canada was $529.79.

Legendre's next bill to the United States treasury covered his cross-country trip from Washington to Santa Fé. Shoemaker accompanied him. In addition to their fare, there is an item of $29.24 for transportation of airplane baggage. The start from Washington was by train, for there is a $2 taxi bill and a $4.50 dinner bill for two on the train. Two days after leaving Washington, or on September 14, Legendre and Shoemaker reached Albuquerque by plane. There they hired an automobile (for which the taxpayers paid $35) to take them to Santa Fé. That afternoon and evening, Legendre and his companion spent $7.50 as miscellaneous expense "incident to entertainment of convention delegates."

The day after their arrival at Santa Fé, Messrs. Legendre and Shoemaker were hosts to ten at luncheon, and to ten again at dinner. Once more—at luncheon the second day after their arrival—ten guests sat down with them at table. The waiters' tips at those three meals were $9. The hotel bill for these two wild life investigators for two days was $136.84. In addition, there was a charge of $15 "miscellaneous expense incident to entertainment of convention delegates" during the two days; a $10 bill paid to a stenographer; tips totaling $6 on leaving the hotel; an automobile charge of $13; tip to porter, $2; and railroad fare on the way to Denver.

Thus two representatives of the committee—no Senators appear to have been present—blew in $246.59 within 48 hours after stepping out of their plane. At the same time, according to Legendre's bill, they were handing Senator Walcott $115.14 to cover his railroad fare and pullman from Chicago to Livingston, Montana, the gateway to Yellowstone Park. While Walcott was looking after wild life in Montana his clerk and special investigator were doing the honors in New Mexico. Both barrels of the expense account were fired at once.

When the convention at Santa Fé ended, Legendre

and Shoemaker headed for the mountains. They went by train to Denver, Casper and Riverton. At Riverton they bought or leased a Ford automobile, paying $81 for the car, a new tire, a jack and a windshield. Gas and oil bills replace railroad charges for a time. The flivver appears to have been decrepit, for within two days after its purchase, the wild life investigators paid another $5 to have it oiled and greased and for gasoline.

Apparently, the newly impressed Ford failed them, for the next day—three days after its purchase or lease—there appear these entries in the expense account: "Service of guide, $12," and "Brakes relined and adjusted on Ford, $10." The same day Legendre paid out $5 in tips for service at hotel, although the name of the hotel is not given. Possibly they had reached Moran, their apparent destination, although this is not clear.

On September 22, their miscellaneous expenses at Moran were $4.50; on the 23rd, miscellaneous expenses incidental to entertainment of committee guests amounted to $9.50 and gas and oil for the Ford were $4 more. On the 24th, they canceled a lunch at the hotel paying $5 therefor and paid $11 for luncheon at Jackson for the committee and guests. The next day, Legendre introduced Senator Norbeck to the expense account with the payment of $19 for the Senator's bill at Teton.

Eighty dollars paid to a court stenographer for four days' services and $29.40 as his traveling fare next appear on the expense account. On September 27, a tip of $5 "to horse wranglers on trip to Mount Leidy." The following day, $3 as a tip "to kitchen service for arranging picnic lunch." Two days later Senator Pittman appears in the expense account with the payment of $5.50 for lunch for "Pittman's party at Turpin Meadow."

During this period, it appears, the party, including Senator Pittman—busy with his own investigating, as will appear in another chapter, but not to busy to lend a hand to a friendly colleague—stayed at Teton Lodge. There were seven in the party, although the names of others than Pittman, Legendre and Shoemaker are not given. The expense account makes this clear. Here are the entries for October 4 and 5:

October 4.

Oil and gas, $3.00.
Lunch for Pittman's party of 5, $6.
Tip to Joe Allen, $20.
Tip to Bruce, $15.
Tip to Pip Crannell, $15.
Tip to Joe's two wranglers, $10.
Tip to Mrs. Braizier (housekeeper), $10.
Check to Mrs. Ward (stenographer at Teton), $152.55.

October 5.

Tips on leaving Moran (over a period of 17 days) for a party of 7——
Jessie, waitress, $20.
Second waitress, $20.
Jimmie (fire and general utility boy), $20.

36

Cook, $10.
First chambermaid, $10.
Second chambermaid, $10.
Miscellaneous expenses connected with leaving, $8.
Lunch at Jackson (Pittman, Woodring and self) $6.
2 tickets and Pullman, Victor to Salt Lake City, $36.80.
Dinner en route to Salt Lake City, $4.
Teton Lodge bill (paid by check), $588.99.

Mr. Legendre's check for $588.99 was more than generous. It covered not only the charges against his immediate party, but the bill of one George Pratt, apparently not connected with the party. The mistake was corrected two months later in another expense account submitted to the treasury by Legendre on which the following entry occurs:

Credit: Mr. George Pratt's bill at Teton Lodge, Wyo., which was by error charged to the Special Committee on Wild Life Resources on vouchers of Nov. 11, 1930, $59.46.

With the tang of the air giving zest to their appetites, Pittman and Legendre remained at the Hotel Utah, Salt Lake City, for three days. Their hotel bill amounted to $89.80 and meals were put down on the expense account at $33.50 additional. On October 9 the two wild life investigators appear to have become the guests of the Bear River Duck Club. When they left on the 11th, they left behind a tip of $5 each for guide, gunman, headman and stenographer.

An overnight trip from Ogden landed Pittman and Legendre beside the Golden Gate (at transportation costs of $94.10) where they met up with Mr. Shoemaker, the special investigator. The night of their arrival at San Francisco, Legendre, Shoemaker and Pittman sat down with guests to a dinner that cost the taxpayers $24.50. The keenness for food engendered by the waters of the Great Salt Lake appears to have been outdone by the mellow tang of the Pacific, for Legendre and Shoemaker spent $15 on one day and $10 on the next for meals and incidentals while in San Francisco.

A swing down to the glories of Southern California was next in this quest for information on wild animal life, although the cost of the trip is not included, save for a single item, in the expense account. That item, excess weight on plane baggage, $9, indicates the manner of their passage. Tips of $5 for maid service, $3 for bellboys and $2 for Pittman's valet likewise appear on the bill for October 18.

Senator Pittman's valet appears to have been most attentive at this period of the wild life investigation, for the very next day (October 19) he was given another tip of $3. Maids and bellboys divided $8 among them during the day and another $10 went to reimburse Senator Pittman for "miscellaneous expenses." A hotel bill of $281.15 (apparently at San Francisco, although not stated) likewise was paid by the taxpayers on this day (October 19), plus an additional hotel bill of $54.90 "for extra night."

Here, it seems, the trip was cut short by Senator Pittman's departure for the East. The Senator left in a hurry. An airplane was chartered (at a cost of $180) to bring the Senator from San Diego to Los Angeles. From Los Angeles the Senator sped East by air to Columbus, Ohio, at a cost of $149, making the day's spendings for airplane transportation $329. Nor was that all; the expense account holds $7 for a taxi to the air field at San Diego, $2 paid in tips on the field, and a taxi charge of $7 from the air field at Los Angeles to the hotel. In addition, Senator Pittman's hotel bill at Los Angeles amounted to $170.46 and that of Legendre and Shoemaker to $135.15.

With Pittman out of the picture, Legendre left Los Angeles at once, buying a transcontinental ticket to Spartanburg, South Carolina, which, with pullman charges, totaled $129.93. During the two days, October 19 and 20, this junket appears to have reached the high-tide of its spendings. In 48 hours, Legendre paid out $1,150.59.

Five hundred and seventy-five dollars a day! Such was the amount the taxpayers were called on to spend for showing these three men a good time in Southern California and speeding them on their Eastward way. Spent cheerfully, in the Nation's service, while the pall of a desperate winter loomed over the country and the lengthened bread-lines grew longer still. A refund of $44.50, credited on the expense account later, cut down the daily spendings, however, to the modest sum of approximately $553 a day.

The long trip from Los Angeles to Spartanburg was pleasantly broken at Lafayette, Louisiana. There Legendre stretched his legs, went on to New Orleans and made a trip by boat to Avery's Island. But not without his usual kindness in tipping those who served him. Five dollars to the engineer, $5 to the steward and $10 to the captain of the boat appear on the record. A few days in Louisiana and the ride to Spartanburg was resumed, finally to fetch up at Washington.

And there, on the second floor of the Senate wing of the Capitol, Legendre presented his bill and was paid off in full for the trip. The bill was $4,568.18.

Chapter IV

A $200-a-day Fishing Trip

In late July when the East and Mid-West simmer and
broil in the summer's heat, nights are cool and sleepful
up near the Canadian Line and Minnesota's fish are
hungry. Connecticut swelters in shimmering heat waves.
St. Louis sweats, and even the hills in distant Nevada,
where the town of Tonopah lies gem-like in rich setting,
warm to the torrid sun. The long dog-days come and go
with little surcease from the heat, and the inflamed
thoughts of men turn naturally to sparkling waters and
cooling winds.

Three minds, it would appear, had but a single thought
in the dying days of July, 1930. One of those minds was
that of Senator Walcott of Connecticut. Another was
that of Senator Hawes of Missouri. The third was the
mind of Key Pittman, Senator from Nevada. The
thought uppermost in those senatorial minds centered
on the wild life with which the numerous fair lakes of
Minnesota abound. And such a thought was not only
natural but in keeping with duty, for the three Senators
had been commanded by the Senate to investigate the
country's wild life and suggest means for conserving it.

41

Hence in the line of duty, Walcott dropped all other affairs at Norfolk, Conn., Hawes relinquished his tasks at St. Louis and Pittman hied himself away from Tonopah. They met at Wabasha, Minnesota, where they had been preceded by Carl Shoemaker, the special investigator of the Senate committee, and soon were joined by Morris Legendre, its secretary.

The story of the ten-day trip is taken from Mr. Legendre's expense account. Here and there the recital is incomplete, leaving enchanting details to the imagination, but in highlight and shadow the picture is well and truly shown by his dispassionate entries. One intriguing bit of information, however, is lacking altogether: nowhere does it appear that a single fish was caught. In fairness to the committee, however, it should be remembered that lack of such information in no wise impaired the legality or validity of the expense account. Mr. Legendre was not required by law to say how many, if any, fish fell victim to the senatorial lure, and he didn't. So one can only wonder what luck befell the party.

Mr. Legendre's expense account opens, as usual, with his departure from Washington. At Chicago he transshipped by train for his Minnesota destination. He left Washington on July 24 and apparently arrived at Wabasha on the evening of the 25th, having telegraphed the waiting group that he was on his way. Indeed, two telegrams appear in the expense account. One was sent to Messrs. Walcott and Shoemaker, but the other is down as having been sent, broadly speaking, simply to Minnesota.

The day after Mr. Legendre's arrival at Wabasha he ran true to form by scattering tips. His expense account contains the following entries for the 26th:

> Tip to cook on boat at Wabasha, $3; to cook's helper, $3; to captain aboard the Wood Duck, $5; to captain's helper, $3; to the porters at Wabasha station, $2.25; and to the man who helped with baggage at Scottt's camp, $1.50.

With this total of $17.75 in tips for the day, Mr. Legendre proceeded to pay off the guides who had served Messrs. Walcott, Pittman, Hawes and Shoemaker before the Legendre arrival. The guides had devoted thirteen days to the party, at $6 a day. To their bill of $78, Mr. Legendre added a modest tip of $5.50.

Almost immediately after his arrival, the party moved on. By train they traveled to Orr, via seven railroad tickets, four single pullman sections and a drawing room, a total of $126.24 in transportation charges. From Orr the group proceeded to Fort Frances where they remained over night at the Rainy Lake Hotel. The next day they hired a motorboat (at a cost of $60) to take them to Crane Lake, pausing at Kettle Falls for luncheon.

That was not quite all, however. There was a need, it seems, for soda, often useful in cases of sunburn, mosquito bite, indigestion, sea-sickness or what have you.

43

Two dollars' worth of soda—sufficient at ordinary prices to encase a towering Senator in an alkali cast—started with the party in the motorboat and, presumably, served its various purposes.

The expense account shows that Crane Lake Hotel was reached that afternoon or night. The next day the four fishermen—one of the party appears to have been left out—inquired into local laws and ordinances and learned that even Senators were required to take out licenses to fish. So they got the licenses, four at $22 for the lot (obligingly paid for out of the United States treasury along with the other expenses of the trip), and invested in certain other things, to-wit:

> Seven mineral waters, $3.50; three sinkers, 15 cents; tips, $4; nine meals and four beds at Lac La Croix, $54; and hotel bill at Crane Lake Hotel, $14.50.

Four guides at $5 a day apiece next appear on the expense account. Apparently, the four guides and the other five in the party ate 48 meals the next day. The entry reads 48 meals at $1 each, $48. If there were but nine in the party—possibly there were more, although it does not appear on the bill—each member ate an average of five and one-third meals that day. It is hard to believe this, but the expense account, of course, is truthful. It carries, too, on that day, a supper charge of $4.

Someone, doubtless with old-fashioned ideas of fishing, hired a canoe. The expense account lists the item at

$1.50. However, the main party stuck to motorboats. There were three of these, at $5 a day apiece.

It is one of the peculiar phenomena of Minnesota's lakes that thirst, torturing and pleasure-killing, is apt to steal at unguarded hours upon those who cast their bait upon the waters. To this general scourge of Nature, even a senatorial fishing party is no exception. Happily, the party appears to have been warned of the danger in time. To meet it, an ample supply of mineral water—the chemical components of which, by ill luck, are not given in the bill—was purchased. The amount of mineral water bought against the danger is put down in the expense account at $31.

It must have been too much mineral water, for the party of nine seems to have slept that night in six beds. That is all the government is charged for—six beds at $1 apiece, $6. Nor was that the only distressing development that followed the purchase of the mineral water, for the next day, instead of three motorboats there appear on the expense account only a solitary canoe and a rowboat. Nobody wanted to fish from a motorboat that day.

However, in other respects the expense account held its own. The following entries, totaling $74.30, cover the day:

> Fifty-one meals, $51; one guide, $5; one canoe, $1.50; can of minnows, 75 cents; one rowboat for three days, $4.50; one tent for four days, $3; eight gallons of oil (whether castor or lubricating is not

45

stated), $4; six mineral waters, $3; one notebook, 15 cents; matches, 15 cents; and one spoon hook, $1.25.

By this time the fishing party appears to have had enough. Any fisherman knows how it is. The bedding situation apparently improved, however, for the expense account of August 1 shows that the party occupied ten beds at $1 apiece and ate eleven breakfasts, also at $1 each. But enough is enough; so they summoned a truck, a school bus and an automobile, and moved, bag, baggage (and let us hope, fish, too) away from Minnesota.

In parting, a tip of $7 was left at Crane Lake Hotel for the cook and his helper. Railroad tickets, homeward bound, were bought; Hawes, Legendre and Shoemaker celebrated with a $9 dinner, and another glorious trip faded into the dimming colors of happy memories.

When the trio reached Chicago somebody appears to have developed intense longing to reach his destination in hot speed. It is unfortunate, for the record, that the identity of this high desire is not disclosed. However, to gratify it, an airplane was chartered for eight hours at $40 an hour; and with the money thus withdrawn from the public treasury the craving was quelled. Somebody rode somewhere by airplane from Chicago and the bill of $320 was paid by the taxpayers.

While Mr. Legendre, as the committee's servant, met the brunt of all charges, the expense account shows there were some bills he did not pay personally. There were expenses, for instance, incidental to bringing Senator Hawes from St. Louis and to Senator Pittman's pilgrimage from Tonopah. These expenses were repaid by Mr. Legendre when the party broke up, as follows:

Senator Walcott $393.12
Senator Hawes 99.23
Senator Pittman 97.56

Jotting down all items, the trip cost the taxpayers $1,-983.67. It lasted ten days, from July 24 to August 3, inclusive. The average spendings from the treasury during that period thus were $198.37 a day. It seems a pity that the taxpayers were not told how many fish the Senators caught.

Leaving Wabasha, Mr. Shoemaker, the special investigator, moved on by automobile to New York by way of Toronto, dropping in there to attend the junket referred to in the preceding chapter. The speedometer on Mr. Shoemaker's car registered 1,612 miles on that part of his trip. Under government regulations he was reimbursed for his transportation at the rate of seven cents a mile. For making the trip from Wabasha to New York he received $124.59, as shown in the voucher he submitted for expenses from July 4 to October. That voucher totaled $1,628.65. And, all told, Mr. Shoemaker drove his car 3,635 miles on the trip.

Not long, however, was the travel-stained investigator

slated to remain at Washington. In a few days he was gone again, this time on a journey that carried him through Santa Fé to Portland, Oregon; to Seattle, San Francisco, Los Angeles, Denver and thence, by easy stages, home. For five long months, Mr. Shoemaker was out in the field, or until December 6th, when the short session of Congress convened. His travels on the second trip, lasting two months, cost $975.18 but not all of this expense was incurred by him personally. A few dollars here and a few dollars there went to defray expenses of other members or employees of the committee.

Mr. Shoemaker's two trips cost the taxpayers approximately $2,600 in expenses plus his salary for five months at $375 a month. Then, with Congress in session and with members of the wild-life committee held to the capital, Shoemaker and Legendre settled down for a time to life in Washington. The tedium was broken by only two out-of-town meetings and a short trip to Florida. In none of these, apparently, did Shoemaker participate. Upon Legendre alone devolved the duty of representing the Senate committee on those occasions.

Yet the humdrum life involved a certain amount of expense at Washington. There was, for instance, the press clipping bureau, engaged at a minimum charge of $5 a month to watch the newspapers and send to the committee such clippings as related to its work. It is significant that the various expense accounts, without exception, carry only the minimum charge for clippings. Apparently the committee's intensive study yielded a crop of not more than 100 newspaper clippings a month. The Senators did not unduly seek the limelight.

Legendre's expense account for December, which totaled $1,090.96, gathered in the loose ends of the Western trip. Among the items was a charge of $54.50 for a camera for use on Senator Pittman's trip in the Wyoming thoroughfare country and pictures of Jackson Hole. Another item covered Senator Pittman's hotel bill at San Francisco. That amounted to $289.53.

The first of the two winter meetings attended by Legendre was the American Game Conference, held at New York, December 9, 10, and 11. Legendre stayed at the Pennsylvania Hotel; his bill for the three days was $165.34. A shorthand expert from Washington presumably went with him, as the expense account contains an item of $59.50 for reporting. The second out-of-town meeting was the Northeastern Game Conference, held at Boston in January. Incidental to that meeting there appears in the expense account a charge of $16.50 for "clerical assistance in Boston in connection with address before the Conference."

The trip to Miami—taken in January—cost the government $161.20. Mr. Legendre notes on the account that only ten of the thirteen days covered by the trip were spent in the committee's service, the other three days being counted as a part of his vacation. "I have therefore charged only ten-thirteenths of entire fare to the government," he notes.

And so the secretary and investigator worked in Washington during the session, staying against the day when Congress should adjourn. On March 4, by Constitutional limitation, Congress did adjourn, and once more wild life beckoned. Not from the bleak and snow-swept Northland did the summons come, but from the rose-covered fields of Georgia, basking in the early spring sunshine.

Five days after Congress adjourned members of the wild-life committee, heading the imperative call from the mellow South, moved on to Georgia. Walcott, Hawes, Norbeck and Pittman, with Legendre going along, of course, boarded a train at Washington on March 9 for the Okefenokee Swamp, near Waycross. The Swamp was not alluring; five days later they were all back in Washington. Nearly half of the time was spent going and coming.

But they saw the Swamp, and, as usual, Legendre scattered tips. The expense account records the chartering of an Eastern Air Transport Company plane for one hour and forty-five minutes to fly over Okefenokee Swamp ($131.25), and the payment of the following tips while at Waycross:

> Tips to servants at hotel, $6; tips to cook and waitress at Hebard's camp, $10; tip to guide at Hebard's camp, $20; miscellaneous tips, meals, etc., $10. Total $46.

The cost of this five-day jaunt to Georgia totaled $654.85 for the party, somewhat more than $130 a day. Three of the four Senators appear to have traveled then enough for the fiscal year—at least on wild-life committee business—but not so the fourth, Hawes of Missouri.

Within a month of the Georgia trip, Hawes was down in the land of cotton again. Shoemaker accompanied him. Their peregrinations took them from Washington to Charleston, S. C., to Jacksonville, to Tallahassee and back again to Washington. Their errand was attendance at a conference of Florida game officials and the inspection of a quail experiment in the vicinity of Thomasville, Georgia. They left Washington April 11 and returned on the 18th. Expenses for the week's trip were $371.30.

There still was other work to do, and Hawes again bent to the yoke. Two days after returning to Washington, or on April 20, he and Shoemaker were off for Chicago to attend the Izaak Walton League convention. They went by way of New York, and reached Chicago on the 22nd. During the three-day convention, the Hawes-Shoemaker hotel bill amounted to $243.38, about $40 a day apiece. On the return home they stopped off in Virginia to visit a certain game farm. Back in Washington they landed April 28, after an absence of eight days, with an expense account totaling $541.90.

And there, so far as the fiscal year goes, the chapter ends. The record shows that the committee spent

$27,361.17 during the year, of which $5,000 was for Legendre's salary, $4,500 was for Shoemaker's, and $3,500 for salaries of two clerks. Thirteen thousand dollars in salaries, and $14,361.17 for railroad fare, pullman charges, tips, airplane flights, hotel bills, tips, auto hire, stenographer hire, guide hire, tips, telegrams, photographs, mineral water, tips, tent hire, boat hire, messenger hire, tips, fishbait, minnows, cigars, tips, taxis, sodas, glasses, tips, lunches, sinkers, canoes, tips, notebooks, matches, pants-pressing, tips, telegrams, telephones and tips.

Every cent of that money came from the federal treasury. Every cent was put in the treasury by the tax-payers.

Was it worth it? What has the public to show now, two years from the time it started, for the expenditure of this money? Nothing; nothing whatever. But, on the other hand, the committee and its henchmen had a wonderful time, even in a dry land. What a time they might have had in a country not under prohibition! There comes to mind a couplet long mouthed around the poker table at the National Press Club in Washington:

> *What! No cheese*
> *To go with these?*

Chapter V

"Hail! Hail! The Gang's All Here!"
(What the hell do we care?)

With scant savings, shortened working time, reduced wages and 5,000,000 unemployed men and women, the United States swung into the second bleak winter of the depression. The glory of a long Indian Summer dimmed to grayness. The chill haze of November days blanketed the growing bread-lines. Fitfully, as spirits await the summons of the Resurrection morning, the hopes of men stirred in the flash of revival promised by the brief holiday pick-up; and then, as Christmas came and passed, settled down again to brave the winter rigors of despair.

A green Christmas marked the dying year at Washington. On Capitol Hill, where shadows of leafless trees fell on still verdant grass below, the halls of both Houses of Congress had echoed high words of hope. Before the twinkling lights of outdoor Christmas trees had danced in youthful eyes, those halls had rung with the brave resolve of the Nation's lawmakers to lead the country out of its encircling gloom. A sobered Congress, grim and resolute, but lately had assembled there.

But something of its grimness faded as the spirit of

Christmas hovered over the despondent land. And now with the coming of The Day itself, those halls were solitary and deserted. The holiday recess emptied the city of its lawmakers, and for the season a moratorium was declared on all things, save hunger, cold and fear.

In this solemn hour of national reflection, a group of statesmen in the United States Senate bethought themselves of fairer days and climes. Of coral strands lapped by turquoise seas. Of sparkling sunshine, of laughter on summer beaches, of whispering palms; maybe, of tinkling music drowsing serenely in the moonlight over untroubled lakes and streams.

To find the setting for these idyllic fantasies, so appealing in the harshness of a raw December, is but a simple chore to those who know well the way to the treasury's back door. To act upon the knowledge is even simpler.

And so, the day after Christmas, the carefree group left behind the gray walls of Union Station, the bare boughs, the winter frost, the suffering and the misery of the unemployed, and sped to Florida. At the expense, let it be noted, of the public purse entrusted to their guarding.

The gay party leaving all these things behind as they sped to the Southland's soft seduction consisted of six Senators and their official guests. The Senators were:

Gerald P. Nye of North Dakota, chairman of the select committee on senatorial expenses who for many

54

months had been engaged in ferreting out possibilities of corruption on the part of candidates for election to the Senate.

Tasker L. Oddie of Nevada, chairman of the important committee on post offices and post roads.

Otis F. Glenn of Illinois.

Henry F. Ashurst of Arizona, ranking Democratic member of the Senate judiciary committee.

Peter Norbeck of South Dakota, chairman of banking and currency, one of the most important of the Senate's committees.

Thomas J. Walsh of Montana whose Teapot Dome revelations will stand long as a warning to the evildoer in public life.

The official guests of the committee were Messrs. A. B. Cammerer, assistant director of the National Park Service; T. G. Pearson, president of the American Audubon Society who came on from New York, at public expense, to Washington to accept the invitation; and E. F. Coe, president of the Everglades Park Association, who apparently welcomed the others on their arrival at Miami and joined the party there. The group of Senators were members of the committee on public lands and surveys, of which Mr. Nye was chairman; and the pretext, or occasion, for their swinging down to Florida over New Year's was an inspection of lands proposed for the making of a new Everglades National Park.

They traveled via the Seaboard Air Line Railway whose bill for the service was paid by the Senate disbursing officer on February 2, about six weeks later. Each member of the party of eight occupied a drawing room or a compartment of a pullman car. This arrangement necessitated the purchase of double railroad fare. The taxpayers thus paid not only for each member's transportation, but paid it twice, both ways. The Seaboard's bill is itemized as follows:

> Sixteen round trip railroad tickets from Washington, D. C. to Miami, Fla., and return, at $41.83 each, $669.28.
> Three drawing rooms from Washington, D. C. to Miami, Fla., at $46.50 each, $139.50.
> Five compartments from Washington, D. C. to Miami, Fla., at $36.75 each, $183.75.
> Four drawing rooms from Miami, Fla., to Washington, D. C., at $46.50 each, $186.00.
> Three compartments from Miami, Fla., to Washington, D. C., at $36.75 each, $110.25.

The total of those items is $1,288.78. It may be noted that eight persons made the trip to Miami and only seven persons made the return trip. That is explained by another entry on the same date covering the payment of $84.70 to Mr. Pearson to reimburse him for railroad fare from New York to Washington, and from Jacksonville back to New York, including meals and incidental expenses.

Thus the transportation charges to the public for this holiday jaunt to Florida totaled $1,373.48. And while the figure appears considerable for taking eight men to Florida and bringing them back to Washington, it was only the beginning of the story.

There was, it seems, a hotel bill of parts. Submitted by the Hotel Pancoast and paid on January 16, the bill itemizes the services rendered (on the American plan) to the various members of the official party as follows:

Senator Gerald F. Nye, Chairman $134.07
Senator Tasker L. Oddie 126.11
Senator Otis F. Glenn 107.64
Senator Henry F. Ashurst 104.70
Senator Peter Norbeck 62.70
Senator Thomas J. Walsh, of Montana .. 30.00
A. B. Cammerer 61.30
T. G. Pearson 61.48
E. F. Coe 79.67
Miscellaneous items for purposes of said
   committee, including preparation of
   fish exhibits 143.50

Total $911.17

(Refunded by the chairman, Senator Nye, $117, covering item erroneously charged for preparation of fish exhibit.)

The party's stay at the hotel was from December 28 to January 3. If both dates are included, eight days were spent at Miami. The per diem hotel expenses of the group ranged from $3.75 a day in the case of Senator Walsh to $16.76 a day in the case of Senator Nye.

Hotel bill and transportation for the merry group during the holiday recess thus mounted to a total cost of $2,284.65.

But there was still more involved. The boundaries and confines of a proposed National Park may not be inspected from the broad piazzas of a winter resort hotel. Closer views are necessary.

So a couple of houseboats were chartered for the party's use. Evidently, the boats (named the *Windswept* and the *Chicot*) were houseboats in keeping with senatorial ideas of a junket at public expense. The bill, submitted by Thomas J. Pancoast and paid out of the United States treasury on January 16, would indicate that the vessels were the last word in luxury. Here it is:

> For charter of houseboats *Windswept* and *Chicot* for use of the Committee on Public Lands and Surveys during its investigation of the location and boundaries of the proposed Everglades National Park in the State of Florida, pursuant to Senate Resolution on May 5, 1930, from December 30, 1930, to January 3, 1931, including oil, gas, guide and pilot service, and incidentals, $1,687.50.

For five days the party of nine used the two houseboats, at an average cost of $337.50 a day, or about $35 a day per person. Meantime, the hotel bill appears to have been accumulating just as if there had been no houseboats.

Anyone who has ever tried to inspect a National Park from the decks of two houseboats knows that certain difficulties lie in the way. The difficulties were anticipated before the houseboats were hired, for the expense account shows that on December 29 the party leased a blimp from which to make overhead inspection. There is no entry to show whether the entire party took the air in the blimp or whether the ascension was undertaken by a sub-committee. In any case, the results of the first day's observations from aloft apparently warranted the hiring of the blimp for a second day.

So on December 30 the party used both the houseboats and the blimp. Of the latter, however, they seem to have wearied soon; the whole nine of them took to the houseboats and hotel on December 31 and again on New Year's Day. For that 48-hour period the blimp does not appear on the federal pay roll. The next day, January 2, it floated into service again, thereby marking the high tide of the junket's spendings with expenses going full blast on earth, on sea and in the air. The hotel bill, the houseboat bill and the blimp bill all were operating simultaneously.

And now the end of the holiday recess neared; in a few days the Senate would resound again with the wisdom of economy and relief. The senatorial party and their

59

guests looked North reluctantly. As the sunny hours ebbed away, they bethought themselves of a token to take with them on their departure, some earnest, perhaps, of their visit.

To obtain this token they hired two photographers and engaged in a transaction involving views of the Everglades. Fourteen pictures were taken. Twelve complete sets were made up, one apiece for everybody and three sets for the folks back in Washington, making 168 pictures altogether. At the nominal cost of one dollar a photograph, the charge on the public purse was $168. Then the party went home, happy and successful. The trip hadn't cost any of them a single cent and they all had enjoyed a wonderful time.

That trip cost the taxpayers a pretty penny, however:

For railroad and pullman fare............	$1,373.48
For hotel accommodations	911.17
For the two houseboats	1,687.50
For the blimp	75.00
For the twelve sets of pictures	168.00
For Senator Oddie, to repay him money he spent on the trip	26.00
For everything	$4,241.15

On their return to Washington, it was rumored that the committee had bought the two houseboats. This baseless report was scotched in the nick of time, before the property custodian had started out to look for the boats and claim them as government property. Explanation was made that the boats had not been bought for the $1,687.50, but simply had been leased a few days, and all was well.

While the distinguished Senators and their guests were holiday-tripping in Florida at public expense, ten thousand men and women in New York City sat down to charity Christmas dinners. The cost of feeding these ten thousand was somewhat less than the forty-two hundred dollars spent by the official party on its trip. Of such stuff is statesmanship made.

Senators think fluently and naturally in terms of hundreds of millions and of billions; a few thousands here and there are as grains of dust in the rarefied air of higher finance engrossing them. Possibly some Senators can't think in terms of hundreds or of thousands at all. So far as this trait applies to junket spendings, there seems to be some justification for the assumption. Yet the human mind is elastic and adaptable; like the eye, it can fix its attention first on the immensity of space with its swimming star-clusters and then observe with equal facility the antics of the microscopic atom. So it is with the senatorial mind; at times it is capable of comprehending the true worth of the smallest of sums. Even a dollar bill is held in esteem when Senators draw their mileage.

In the Senate there are masters of the art of spending public funds gracefully and fast. The touch of their fingers sprouts wings on money. Into any of at least a dozen senatorial hands Uncle Sam could cram a bundle of thousands secure in the faith that tomorrow there would be not a dime remaining. Many Senators are big-hearted that way. And some of them possess hidden talents for making their spendings come out exactly even with what they are privileged to draw from the treasury.

There is, for instance, the case of Senator Pittman of Nevada. When Senator Pittman starts out to spend ten thousand dollars, he spends ten thousand dollars, no more and no less. There is no odd change left. Nor is there any over-spending. The Senator believes, too, that Senators should work for the public weal during their vacations.

Four weeks before the ending of the regular session of Congress in July, 1930, the Senate adopted a resolution to investigate treaties and trade relations between the United States and China. The investigation was to be undertaken by the foreign relations committee. That committee appointed a sub-committee to do the actual investigating, and of the sub-committee, Pittman was chairman.

Now an investigation of treaties and trade relations between the United States and China is not the sort of thing calculated to splash scare heads into the newspapers. Nevertheless as a summer chore for a Senator eager to go it will suffice. So it served Senator Pittman. The expense account shows that with Senators Swanson of Virginia and Shipstead of Minnesota, Senator Pittman held his investigation on the Pacific Coast. Hearings were held in August and September at San Francisco, Los Angeles and Seattle.

At San Francisco the three Senators established headquarters at the Fairmount Hotel. The bill rendered by and paid to the Fairmount was $1,085.95. It covered approximately two weeks.

At Los Angeles the committee established headquarters at the Ambassador Hotel. On September 15, they paid the Ambassador's bill, covering about one-half month. The amount was $2,221.82.

At Seattle, the Olympic Hotel was the committee headquarters. One week after paying the Ambassador Hotel bill at Los Angeles, the committee paid the Olympic Hotel bill at Seattle. The Olympic bill was $1,379.62.

For hotel bills during a period of five weeks and two days, the expense account of those three Senators amounted to $4,687.39, or at the rate of about $900 a week. That is going fairly fast, even for United States Senators on vacation.

The hotel bills are not itemized, so there is found in them none of the intriguing detail disclosed by the entries of the committee on wild animal life, in whose duties Senator Pittman also participated during the vacation period. To the contrary, the entries are brief and businesslike. They come immediately to the point with the totals; and they demonstrate Senator Pittman's almost uncanny ability to spend exactly ten thousand dollars on a given task—not a dime less, not a dollar more.

Here is the Pittman bill for inquiring into the state of American business with China, as it appears on pages 120 and 121 of Senate Document No. 1, the annual report of the Secretary of the Senate:

August 12. To salary Raymond A. Walsh, assistant to chairman, July 19 to Aug. 18, 1930 ....$ 600.00

August 12. To expenses Raymond A. Walsh, assistant to chairman, in connection with hearings on the Pacific Coast.........   500.00

August 16. To C. F. Pace for railroad tickets to San Francisco for committee hearings 209.96

August 16. To Claude A. Swanson for expenses in connection with hearings on Pacific Coast 400.00

August 27. To Henrik Shipstead for expenses in connection with hearings on Pacific Coast 227.74

August 30. To payment Hotel Fairmount bill (San Francisco) in connection with committee expenses for period of hearings in San Francisco 1,085.95

Sept. 12. To Raymond A. Walsh, assistant to chairman, for expenses incident to hearings on coast 400.00

Sept. 12. To Raymond A. Walsh, assistant to chairman, salary from Aug. 19 to Sept. 18, 1930 ....   600.00

Sept. 15. To Henrik Shipstead for expenses incident to hearings on Pacific Coast   100.00

64

Sept. 15. To payment Ambassador Hotel bill (Los Angeles) in connection with committee expenses during period of hearings in Los Angeles 2,221.82

Sept. 22. To payment of Hotel Olympic bill for committee during period of hearings in Seattle 1,379.62

Oct. 17. To Raymond A. Walsh, assistant to chairman, salary from Sept. 19 to Oct. 18, 1930 .... 600.00

Nov. 15. To Raymond A. Walsh, assistant to chairman, salary from Oct. 19 to Nov. 18, 1930 .... 600.00

Nov. 28. To Stever, Smith & Jones, official stenographers, for taking testimony Los Angeles hearings 320.85

Nov. 28. To A. T. Petty, official reporter, for taking testimony during San Francisco hearings 327.80

Nov. 28. To Eagan Ridenour, official stenographer, for taking testimony of Seattle hearings 124.45

Nov. 28. *To reimburse self for expenses incident to and in connection with trip and hearings on Pacific Coast, and 2 trips to New York City* 301.81

Total $10,000.00

The last entry (which does not appear in italics in the official report) is mute evidence of Senator Pittman's skill in making things come out even. Some persons acquire this knack early in life, as boys, perhaps, at their fathers' dining tables. Others acquire it in the United States Senate, and still others never do acquire it. How and when Senator Pittman acquired it is not stated in the dry record. Only his possession of the knack is shown. After paying off everybody else in connection with the hearings, there remained a sum of $301.81; it was just enough to reimburse the Senator for what he had spent. And thus the total spendings came to an even ten thousand dollars.

But whatever gratification Senator Pittman may have felt over balancing his committee budget was doomed to short life, for the next day the disbursing clerk was called on to pay another Pittman bill of $265 as a balance due Senator Pittman incidental to the trip. Nor was that the last of the pay-off man's dealings with the how's-business-with-China committee. On December 18, Mr. Walsh, Pittman's assistant, was around for his month's salary of $600, and that, too, was paid. Then for six months no further bill from this committee was submitted.

The fiscal year had almost closed when Senator Pittman's next bill came along. Like the ten-thousand dollar bill, it was brief and to the point. Here is the way it appears in the record:

> June 18. For amount expended as chairman of the sub-committee of the Committee

on Foreign Relations investigating treaties
and trade relations with China, under resolution of June 2, 1930, the same having been
advanced on Apr. 15, by the Secretary of the
Senate, under provisions of the deficiency act
of Mar. 3, 1879 ....$8,387.39

That was all. No items. No hotel bills. No railroad
fare. No stenographers' fees. No detail whatever. Of
the ingredients that composed the $8,387.39 confection the
public will remain forever in ignorance. It has Senator
Pittman's word that the money was spent—which nobody
doubts, of course—and that alone must suffice.

Thus during a year when the deficit in the treasury
crept toward the billion-dollar mark, when an approach-
ing mammoth increase in federal taxes cast its shadow
over the land, nearly twenty thousand dollars of the public
funds were pleasantly blown in to ascertain the status of
our treaties and business relations with China.

One hopes that the Senator found the China trade
flourishing. Somewhere on this twirling sphere of mud
we call the globe business really ought to be good, and,
maybe, China is the place.

Chapter VI

Small-fry Junkets and Page One

There are more ways of killing a cat than kissing it to death. And there are many ways of financing a senatorial vacation out of the United States Treasury. Investigating wild life is one way; looking into our business with China is another; holiday-tripping to Florida is a third. All these are pretty good, but they hardly scratch the surface of possibilities. In far-flung America there are so many things to investigate and so many places to visit that even a dull-witted Senator has little difficulty in making a choice. All he has to do is to use the gray matter Heaven put under his bald spot.

One of the things that certainly needed looking into during the summer of 1930 was the Alaskan Railway. It hadn't been investigated for a long time. Summer days are long and pleasant in Alaska; there is a chance, too, that one may see the Northern lights. And, of course, it is desirable that a Senator should see things in every light, including the Northern. Besides, a pleasant boat trip is involved. Other trips had become a bit passé; but when one goes to Alaska, one goes somewhere.

Preparedness is necessary for a senatorial vacation on a

federal expense account. The trip to Alaska barely squeaked through; the Senate didn't adopt the authorizing resolution till July 1, 1930, two days before Congress adjourned. On the day the Senate did adopt the resolution, however, the vacationists dispatched a man from Los Angeles to Seattle, presumably to clear the way for their pilgrimage. His transportation is down in the expense account at $61.71, and the date of the entry is July 1.

Why should the Senate send a committee to Alaska? Evidently it occurred to the Senate that some spoil-sport might ask that question. The answer is given in the resolution. The Alaskan Railway, constructed and owned by the United States, needed investigation as to its "operation, its economic situation, and its prospects!" Here, Howell, you run up to Alaska—at public expense—and see what the prospects are! So commanded the Senate. And Howell obeyed, Howell of Nebraska.

With him went Kendrick of Wyoming and John Thomas of Idaho. The junket started early in August and by mid-September it was all over except paying the bills. The total cost to the taxpayers was $4,360.54. It was a moderate charge, as junkets go, covering, as it did, not only the expenses of the three Senators but of several federal workers as well. In Alaska, the expense account indicates, the Senators were accompanied by Admiral R. E. Coontz of the Navy.

The itemized expense account turned in by Senator Howell holds little of unusual interest. Much of the money purchased railroad transportation, food and lodging. Entries indicate that the committee used the services of the U. S. S. *Perry* and the U. S. S. *Wasmuth* on the trip. One of the items, $34, covers a dinner at Vancouver on the committee's return from the Territory. Another, $844.67, covered expenses and compensation at $7 a day for fifty days of Frank A. Harrison, an examiner in the committee's service. A third item, $120 for airplane service at Mount McKinley, indicates that Senators Thomas and Kendrick went aloft for a birdseye view of the railway's prospects.

Before starting on the trip, Senator Howell had the foresight to purchase $143.55 worth of photographic supplies from the Eastman Kodak Stores, Inc., at Omaha. At Anchorage, one of the longest stops, the party stayed five days at the Anchorage Hotel and the bill amounted to $225. That was at the rate of $45 a day, but as there were at least five in the party—the expense account does not make clear just how many there were—it seems apparent that the hotel follows a let-live policy. All told, the trip to Alaska cost the government less than $1,500 per Senator for the three Senators that made it.

For a quiet, bargain-price vacation, attracting little attention but affording a good time, the Alaska trip has many advantages. In addition, it has the distinction of being somewhat original. Not everybody can think up one like that. There are some Senators, for instance, who follow the trite vacation practice of inspecting national parks. That's old stuff. No originality.

It is somewhat surprising, therefore, to find this well-worn track followed by Senator Oddie of Nevada in the summer of 1930. Of an outstanding statesman the country expects more originality, better vacation plans. In taking such a vacation, the Senator appears to have been not up to par. Nevertheless, four days after the ending of the Senate's special session, or on July 26, Senator Oddie started from Washington. He had already drawn his mileage for going home from Washington to Nevada when the Senate session ended, but the expense account shows the start was made from Washington. His inspection, which extended to Alaska, continued until September 1.

Here is the expense account he turned in to the Senate disbursing officer on October 3, receiving prompt payment therefor:

Railroad and pullman transportation, Washington, D. C. to Seattle, Wash., via Glacier National Park, Mont.	$ 209.99
Seward to Fairbanks, Alaska	31.05
Chitma to Cordova, Alaska	15.60
Seattle, Wash. to Reno, Nev., via San Francisco	84.31
Steamship ticket from Seattle, Wash. to Seward, Alaska, and return	254.00
Extra for stateroom on return trip to Seattle, Wash.	30.00

Automobile hire and driver, and expenses for 8 days	120.00
Clerical assistant during course of trip....	8.00
Hotel accommodations	204.82
Meals	46.25
Tips, porterage, baggage, telegrams and taxicabs	95.25
Total	$1,099.27

Another small-fry junket that was not authorized until late in the session (May 14, 1930) carried Senator Frazier of North Dakota to Lo, the poor Indian. As chairman of the Committee on Indian Affairs, Senator Frazier sought first-hand information. Living conditions and the white man's treatment of Lo and his wife were the North Dakota Senator's especial concern. The expense account, submitted and paid December 11, shows that the trip was made in Indian Summer when the climatic conditions in Mississippi, Texas and Oklahoma, where he went, were at their best.

Senator Frazier's expense account scorns such trivial details as specific items. It likewise forbears to disclose the identity of the Senators, if any, who junketed with him. It gives broadly only dates, purpose, things paid for, destinations and amounts. Here it is, as spread on the official record:

Nov. 4–25. For reimbursement for expenses incurred as chairman of the Committee on Indian Affairs investigating Indian conditions, under resolution of May 14, 1930: Traveling expenses of self and other members of the committee for railroad fare, pullman charges, hotel accommodations, taxi fares, automobile hire, telephone charges, meals en route, and incidentals from their respective homes and return to same and to the various cities and other points where sessions of the committee were held for the purpose of taking testimony of witnesses and observation of conditions, including Philadelphia, Miss.; Livingston, Tex.; Durant, Idabel, Wewoka, Okmulgee, Muskogee, Miami, Pawhuska, Ponca City, Pawnee, Shawnee, El Reno, Anadarko, and Lawton, all in Oklahoma $1,777.29

Told in a minimum of sentences and detail, but sufficient for the pay-off man. Senator Frazier's brevity, however, was not shared in full by the clerk of the committee, one Nelson A. Mason, who later identified the junketing Senators in a bill covering their expenses from March 17 to June 13. Mr. Mason names them:

> Frazier of North Dakota
> Wheeler of Montana
> Thomas of Oklahoma
> Ashurst of Arizona
> Bratton of New Mexico
> Steiwer of Oregon

Mr. Mason's bill to the taxpayers, paid on June 23, reads as follows:

> For reimbursement for expenses incurred as clerk to the Committee on Indian Affairs making a survey of Indian conditions, under authority of resolution of Feb. 17, 1931, from March 17, 1931 to June 13, 1931—
> Railroad fares, pullman charges, automobile hire and other transportation charges; meals en route, hotel accommodations for rooms; meals at hotels, and subsistence in towns, cities, and Indian agencies visited during a trip of investigation, for Senators Frazier, Wheeler, Elmer Thomas, Ashurst, Bratton, and Steiwer, members of said committee, and for self and special assistants to the committee, Grorud and Milburg; the trip above mentioned having started from Washington, D. C., to Riverside, Calif., thence to 37 Indian agencies located in the States of California, Nevada, New Mexico, Colorado, Arizona, Oregon and Washington $4,812.45

There's the picture. Six distinguished Senators, each of whom had received his mileage home from Washington at the close of the session on March 4 (at four times what the necessary traveling expenses really amounted to); a start from Washington thirteen days later; a trip to California at public expense.

It was cold, raw and disagreeable in the North, but the six Senators knew about it only by hearsay as they enjoyed life—at the taxpayers' expense—in Southern California. Thence they flit to the balmy airs of Arizona, New Mexico, Nevada, Colorado; and then to Oregon—the land of Roses—and the state of Washington.

All, girls and boys, at your expense and mine and the other taxpayers' of the United States. It was a sweet little trip that cost only $800 or so per Senator. The resolution under which they flitted, feasted and frolicked was adopted by the Senate just two weeks before Congress adjourned. The suspicion grows that it may have been adopted to give these gentlemen a good time out of the public treasury.

It was not the same resolution under which Senator Frazier had made his earlier swing around the Indian clubs at a cost of $1,777.29. There were two resolutions. The resolution of May 14, 1930, was the $1,777.29 resolution and the resolution of February 17, 1931, was the $4,800 beauty. However, as they were on the same subject, it is permissible, perhaps, to put them down together, thus:

Indian junket No. 1 .... $1,777.29
Indian junket No. 2 .... 4,812.45
————————
Two Indian junkets in the fiscal year,
1931 .... $6,589.74

Nor is it shown that the Senators whose identity is cloaked by Senator Frazier's expense account for the $1,777.29 were the same as those whose junketing was proclaimed by Mr. Mason's bill for the $4,812.45. Only the identity of the second junketeers is known.

Not all Senate investigations, the expense account discloses, fall into the class of junkets. Some have as their objective not a pleasant vacation at government expense but Page One of the newspapers. Page One is regarded as a great asset to a Senator; greatest when the Senator's term is nearing the day of prospective renewal. To make Page One, however, it generally is necessary that the subject investigated have a universal appeal; or, lacking such appeal, that hearings speedily develop sensational testimony. Only then can an investigation roost on a scare-head.

The Teapot Dome investigation is an illustration. At first there was nothing about it to excite the man in the street. And of all subjects, oil is the prosiest. The investigation dribbled along for weeks without raising an eyebrow. Senator Walsh, chairman of the committee, was so discouraged he thought seriously of closing up shop and calling it a day. Then came redemption: the Fall-Doheny-Sinclair testimony, the little black bag and other hot developments. The show became a wow overnight; just another Senator became a national hero.

Sensational evidence turned the trick, although the general appeal of the subject investigated grew when it developed that the nation's oil preserves were threatened. But as a subject for senatorial investigation oil was not so good. Bread is a much better subject. Everybody knows what bread is; its circulation is general. The dullest moron has self-interest in bread. Why not investigate it?

The question suggested itself early in 1931. At that time the price trend of virtually everything sold over the counter was downward. Farm products had plummeted to almost unbelievable depths. They were to fall more but at that time a further decline seemed hardly possible. Meats, eggs, milk, butter—in fact, virtually everything on the dining table—had dropped precipitately. Yet somehow the price of bread seemed to stay aloft.

The astute mind of Senator Capper of Kansas sensed cause for a Senate investigation in the continuing high price of bread. Why, it was asked, with wheat selling at 60 cents a bushel (wheat was then doomed to fall to thirty cents in the months ahead) and with flour selling at from $4 to $5 a barrel, why, under those circumstances, shouldn't bread prices fall to five cents a loaf?

The Senate authorized an investigation. A committee headed by Senator Capper undertook it.

To determine why bread was not selling for five cents a loaf Senator Capper's committee employed two experts at $50 a day apiece. Not two experts on bread, but two experts on working up data for a Senate investigation. One of the experts, Basil Manly of Washington, drew

77

pay for only ten days' work; the next day he experted over to another Senate committee where a longer term lay ahead. That was the Nye committee, investigating the campaign expenditures of candidates for the United States Senate, whose Gargantuan spendings will be related presently. Mr. Manly left his $50-a-day job with Senator Capper to take on a $40-a-day job with Senator Nye.

The remaining expert, C. V. Maudlin, stuck with Senator Capper. Mr. Maudlin became chief investigator for the Capper committee and worked up the committee's case. His bill was submitted and paid out of the treasury on March 3, 1931. Here it is, as shown on the record:

> For services as chief investigator rendered the sub-committee of the Committee on Agriculture and Forestry investigating reasons for the inflexibility of the retail prices of food, under resolution of Jan. 16, 1931, from Jan. 30 to Mar. 4, 1931 (worked all Sundays and holidays) 34 days at $50 per day $1,700.00
>
> Reimbursement of salaries paid assistants as follows:
>
> Arthur Sturgis, investigator, Feb. 4 to Mar. 2, 1931 (worked all Sundays and holidays except Sunday, March 1) 26 days at $35 per day 910.00
>
> Basil M. Manly, expert, Jan. 28 to Feb. 7, 1931, 10 days, at $50 per day 500.00

Arthur Sturgis, Jr., assistant investigator,
Feb. 4 to 28, 1931 (worked all Sundays and
holidays) 25 days at $10 per day 250.00
Georgianna M. Crowther, clerk and typist,
Jan. 30 to Mar. 3, 1931, 4 2/3 weeks, at $35
per week 163.33

Total $3,523.33

The two experts at $50 a day, the investigator at $35
and the investigator's junior at $10, along with the stenog-
rapher at $35 a week, place the spendings at about
$150 a day. To their bill of $3,523.33 must be added the
bill of the expert stenographers who took down the testimony during the ten-day hearings. An original transcript
and two carbon copies were furnished and the bill was
$531.30—somewhat more than $50 a day for the official
reporters.

Thus the total cost of the inquiry exceeded $4,000. The
investigation set no river ablaze so it ended just prior to
the ending of Congress itself, on March 4. In somewhat
more than a month it cost the taxpayers somewhat more
than $4,000. And the price of bread stayed where it was
until the workings of another law which the Senate can
neither repeal nor stay brought it down.

Another Senate investigation frankly aimed at Page
One was kept alive during the entire fiscal year under
the chaperonage of Senator Blaine of Wisconsin. That
was the investigation of post-office leases and rentals.

Hayden of Arizona and Hebert of Rhode Island served with Blaine on the committee. As an illustration of an obscure method of spending thousands of dollars from the public treasury its workings are worthy of examination.

The expense account shows that the committee started the fiscal year with a force of four employees. Of these, John G. Holland, general counsel at $450 a month, topped the pay roll. The secretary of the committee received $200 a month and two women clerks received $125 and $150, respectively.

That was in July, 1930. The pay roll for August shows that both clerks had received a raise in salary to $175 a month. Mr. Holland's raise did not materialize until November, when he received $500. He remained on the committee's pay roll at that figure for the remainder of the fiscal year, except during the month of March when he appears in the Secretary's listing as the employee of another committee. That may have been an error in the entry; April entries show Mr. Holland back on the Blaine committee pay roll at his customary stipend.

Early in August the committee appears to have opened employment negotiations with another attorney. On September 22 the negotiations led to this attorney's making a trip to Boscobel, Wis., Senator Blaine's home. On November 5, the attorney, Fred M. Wylie, received payment from the treasury to cover the expenses of the trip and his services for six and three-quarter days at $20 a day. In October Mr. Wylie was on the pay roll for $525, covering a full month's work. He also submitted an expense account amounting to about $300 during the month.

Mrs. Wylie joined him on the pay roll in October as a typist at $4 a day. In December the Wylies, Mr. and Mrs., drew $794.17 from the treasury to cover services and expenses. The husband's services were at the rate of $20 a day and the wife's at $4. No payments appear to have been made to either during November.

But there had been other additions to the pay roll in the meantime. One was the case of a temporary employee who received $71 for services in October; another concerned a fixture for more than six months. The latter was Donald R. Heggy, an investigator, who entered the committee's service at $300 a month on September 22 and remained on the pay roll until April 15. Thereafter, Heggy worked for 24 days at $10 a day. During the entire period of his employment he traveled considerably, receiving payment for his expenses up to nearly $300 a month additional.

There was nothing spectacular or sensational in the salaries and allowances paid these employees, nor, so far as that is concerned, in their work. Yet October, the high tide of the pay roll spendings, found the following employees of the committee drawing salaries:

John G. Holland, counsel $500
Fred M. Wylie, attorney 525
Mrs. Wylie, typist (14 days) 52
Donald R. Heggy, investigator 300
George Oliver, secretary 200
Lydia H. Finch, clerk 175
Leila Yawn, clerk 175

The seven employees, regular and extra, drew $1,927 in salaries during the month. The committee had not started then to hold hearings. The entire effort to that date appears to have centered on developing evidence to bring out at the subsequent public hearings.

The first of these was held in Chicago. Starting November 12, it continued for three days. The committee then went to St. Paul where another three-day hearing was held. To cover traveling and other expenses of the three Senators, Blaine submitted a bill of $404.83. Measured by the highfalutin charges of certain other committees, the bill was a paragon of modesty.

Back to Washington the committee traveled, and counsel, secretary and investigator started working up material for the second hearing. Two and one-half months apparently were needed for the task. The second batch of hearings was held at Washington. They covered seven days, strung out from February 5 to 20, inclusive. Then followed a period of more than two months before the third, and final, group of hearings during the fiscal year. Those hearings were held at Chicago April 28 to 30, inclusive.

Between hearings fairly numerous small expense accounts were paid as the committee's employees traveled from city to city, developing situations and evidence.

Sixteen days thus were devoted to actual hearings. On those sixteen days, Senator Blaine had the satisfaction of beholding his name on numerous front pages. The committee disclosed conditions shot through with some amount of spice, but except locally the sensations were rather mild. The hearings disclosed nothing comparable to the startling exposures of the Teapot Dome investigation; while the Blaine investigation unearthed sufficient material to prevent its falling into the class of publicity failures, it could hardly be termed a publicity bell-ringer.

Yet the expense to the treasury of continuing the Blaine committee during the fiscal year, according to the various entries in the Senate disbursing clerk's accounts, was $21,552.91. The fees paid the expert stenographers for reporting the sixteen days' hearings, plus the stenographers' essential expenses, amounted to $2,096.48. In the six days of hearings at Chicago and St. Paul in November, the stenographer's fee was $1,060.36. The usual rate of 25 cents for each 100 words recorded and transcribed was paid. For each carbon copy an additional fee of 5 cents per 100 words was paid, and the committee bought five carbon copies.

As the year's efforts of the committee centered on the

hearings, the entire year's expense of about $21,500 may be apportioned with propriety among them. Thus it develops that this obscure special committee spent, on that basis, about $1,350 in preparing for and holding each of the hearings. It hit the First Page at a cost of about $1,350 a day. As the fiscal year ended, the committee's organization was still intact, although the investigator and one clerk at $175 a month had been dropped from the pay roll.

Was the publicity fishing excursion worth it? Possibly it was, to Senator Blaine. The personal cost to him was nothing. As to whether the sixteen hearings were worth $1,350 apiece to the taxpayers, who footed the bills, opinions naturally will vary.

Chapter VII

Lawmakers or Law Violators?

On February 26, 1931, Senator J. Thomas Heflin of Alabama, whose tubby form soon was to shed the senatorial toga, rose to address the Senate.

Senator Heflin's eye went, as usual, to the press gallery. Often before had he raised both eye and voice to the men and women sitting there. "Little squirrel-heads," he had called them. And they had called him "windbag," "pompous," "bombastic" and other unkind terms in their occasional references to him and his fervid oratory. Between Heflin and the press gallery love had not been misplaced. There had been times when his starting to talk had emptied the press gallery enthusiastically of everybody except the press association men held by duty to their seats throughout the session. But not so today; on the chance that the Alabama Senator had risen to sing his swan song, the reporters enthusiastically remained.

It was not to sing, but to fight, that the Senator took the floor. In his hand he held a petition—his own. It was a recital of alleged wrongs, irregularities and frauds. Through those methods, he charged, he had been de-

85

feated for reelection. But for those methods he then would be looking happily forward to another term. Instead, Mr. Bankhead, his opponent in the recent election, had been declared the winner. The verdict, Senator Heflin continued, was unfair, unjust and illegal; and he petitioned his fellow Senators to investigate the election and undo the wrong.

A resolution to investigate was introduced. Two days later, on February 28, the resolution was adopted. Twenty-five thousand dollars were appropriated to defray the expenses of the investigation.

Obviously, the investigation was to be undertaken during the adjournment of Congress. It was then February 28; on March 4 at noon, the session would end by Constitutional limitation. Only four days of life remained in the Seventy-first Congress. Such an investigation would extend over months. The most that Senator Heflin could expect was action favorable to him upon the convening of the next session the following December.

The investigation and the $25,000 were assigned to the Committee on Privileges and Elections. The committee delegated the task and the money to a sub-committee headed by Senator Hastings of Delaware on which Bratton of New Mexico and George of Georgia also served. Thus on March 4 when the hands of the Senate clocks pointed to noon and the Vice-President's gavel fell, signalizing the end of the session, Messrs. Hastings, Bratton and George found themselves with $25,000 and a job.

They also found themselves facing the following provision of the law:

> Senate resolutions providing for inquiries and investigations shall contain a limit of cost of such investigations, which limit shall not be exceeded except by vote of the Senate authorizing additional amounts.

That law was five years old. It was passed in 1926 as a proviso in one of the deficiency bills, and was approved March 3 of that year. Its meaning was clear and unmistakable; the $25,000 and no more was to be spent until the Senate should authorize additional spendings. And the Senate was not to meet again for nine months. Twenty-five thousand dollars was all the committee was authorized to spend during the ensuing nine months; to spend more would violate the law.

Other Senators in other days had found the law a barrier thwarting cherished plans. One Senator, nevertheless, had gone ahead with his spendings, law or no law, incurring obligations on the chance that the Senate subsequently would make good his commitments. Later that Senator had gone hat in hand to make his peace with his fellows—and to get the deficiency grudgingly, with a warning. Another Senator, engaged in an investigation riveting the country's attention had been brought up roundly to a stop sudden and complete when the last dollar of the appropriation had been spent. And still other Senators had been checked in their spendings by the provision. Its presence on the statute books and its unequivocal meaning were known well to every man in the Upper Chamber.

And so, not long after adjournment, the Hastings sub-committee began the Bankhead-Heflin investigation. Its first act, according to the official record of its spendings, was to deposit $3,000 with the postmaster at Washington to cover mailing of the ballots from Alabama to the capital. Why they were sent by mail instead of being forwarded more cheaply by express does not appear. It does appear, however, that $3,000 was too much postage. Every ballot cast for Senator in Alabama in the 1930 election was carried through the mails for less than one-half of the $3,000; the postmaster later refunded $1,789.30 to the committee.

A man was sent to Alabama to impound the ballots. An assistant followed him. While they were in the field, the sub-committee cast about for an expert investigator. From another committee—that headed by Senator Nye—it obtained the services of F. H. Creech. Mr. Creech had a good record with the Nye committee. Senator Nye lent his services for a time to Senator Hastings. Mr. Creech was transferred to the Hastings committee pay roll at $500 a month (his customary pay) and expenses. He remained there about five weeks. During that time he made a trip to Alabama and return and submitted an expense account of $241.39.

88

The nucleus of a clerical organization next was gathered by the Hastings committee. Harrison W. Smith was appointed chief supervisor at $390 a month. Another Smith —William B., Jr.,—was appointed assistant supervisor at the same salary. Two clerks, at $175 and $150, were added. Other assistant supervisors and clerks were added later.

Early in April the two Smiths and Creech left Washington for Alabama. They were absent nine days from the capital and submitted expense accounts totaling $642.40 on their return. From Albuquerque came Senator Bratton and from Georgia came Senator George. Their expenses totaled $427.60. The investigation was beginning to move and the $25,000 was beginning to melt. During April the committee's pay roll expenditure amounted to $3,379.

Early in May the actual count of the disputed ballots was begun with the United States treasury paying all bills and charges. Here a new spending element was introduced. Heflin wanted a lawyer to protect his interests. Bankhead, of course, would have to have a lawyer, too, if Heflin had one. So the committee, following custom, decided to give each claimant a lawyer. Heflin selected Horace A. Wilkinson of Birmingham; Bankhead designated R. B. Evins. Messrs. Wilkinson and Evins were paid by the committee—$250 a month apiece. Their combined pay only equaled that of Mr. Creech, the investigator, but such as it was the treasury provided it. Five hundred dollars a month was added to the committee pay roll.

Thus with the two lawyers drawing $500 a month, the two Smiths drawing $780 a month, the two clerks now drawing $358 a month, the Nye committee investigator, Creech, drawing $500 a month, and six assistant supervisors drawing $1,438 a month, the committee built up an overhead of $3,576 a month before counting a ballot. Early in May, with that overhead, the counting began. The men who did the actual counting received $6 a day apiece; twenty-seven of them worked from seven to ten days apiece during the first fortnight of May.

A pay roll was made out for the counters and on it were placed, as well, some of the clerks and the assistant supervisors, except William B. Smith, Jr., who received his compensation direct from the Senate disbursing officer. For the first half of May the pay roll, representing the bulk of the committee's spendings for salaries and wages, amounted to $2,216. As the committee warmed to its task, the force grew and the pay roll mounted:

First half of May	$2,216
Second half of May	2,486
First half of June	2,744
Second half of June	3,055

In the meantime, other expenses rolled in. Among them was a fee to a handwriting expert, whose exact service to the committee is not disclosed in the bill. A great many photostats were made; one bill for the service amounted to $890.40 and in addition there was a charge of $44.90 for photostat paper. These and other expenses were met out of the dwindling $25,000 fund appropriated by the Senate to carry the committee through.

During June the tempo quickened. The committee's various pay rolls crept up to $7,079 for the month, as follows:

Counters, clerks, assistant supervisors:
First half of June $2,744
Second half of June 3,055
The two Smiths and other employees 1,280

Between February 28, when the $25,000 was appropriated, and June 30, when the fiscal year ended, the committee's spendings totaled $22,185.75. As the new fiscal year dawned, July 1, the committee had left to its credit with the Senate disbursing officer only $2,814.25. It was not enough to last two weeks at the rapid rate at which the investigation was steaming ahead.

At that point, unfortunately for this recital, the curtain falls on the committee's spendings. The annual report of the Secretary of the Senate details spendings each year only until July 1. To read the record of the committee's spendings subsequent to June 30, 1931, one must await the next annual report—and that will not be made available to the public until Congress meets in December, 1932.

So, as this is written, it cannot be told officially that the committee incurred obligations in excess of $25,000. Yet the committee was going ahead fast—at the rate of $7,079 a month—with its task. Did it stop all work when the $25,000 was exhausted? Did it say, "We've spent the $25,000 and now, under the law, we must spend no more"?

It did not. The count continued, though there was not a dollar available in the United States treasury to pay the counters, the clerks, the assistant supervisors, the supervisor, the investigator, the two lawyers, or others. The work went on, but not a nickel more than $25,000 actually was paid out. There was a splendid reason for that: the disbursing officer cannot incur an overdraft. The bills lay unpaid, so far as the treasury was concerned, while the work continued.

In the official record there is nothing to show as yet how the employees got their wages and salaries. Two courses were open: the employees could continue the work and wait till December on the chance that the Senate then would appropriate more money to pay them for the labor already performed; or members of the committee, or friends of the committee, or other persons could advance the money to meet pay rolls. Those guarantors thus would take the chance of reimbursement instead of the clerk and others. Officially, however, the record does not show what course was followed.

In either event, it was physically impossible for the committee to tap the treasury at that time for more than

$25,000. Their access to the treasury lay through the Senate disbursing officer and he could draw only the amount of the appropriation. But there was nothing to stay the committee from running counter to the spirit of the law by incurring indebtedness greater than $25,000. Such a debt would not be collectible at law, for in incurring it the committee would exceed its authority. Those to whom the money was owing could only hope to collect through the good graces of the Senate later; should the Senate's graces subsequently prove not so good, they, the creditors, would be out of pocket and out of recourse as well.

But by all the tenets of decent dealings such a debt would be binding morally on the treasury. Thus while the committee could not exceed the actual spending of $25,000 it could incur an indebtedness morally, if not legally, binding upon the taxpayers.

And that is precisely what the committee did. Restricted to the spending of $25,000, it spent the money and then went in debt. By what authority? Certainly by no authority whatever, so far as the laws of the United States disclose. By authority, perhaps, of good fellowship in the Senate and the discretion of the committee members. An authority like a borrower's hope on entering a bank; a bit stronger, perhaps, because in the Senate, where everyone knows everyone else as a pretty good fellow and the rule is you-do-for-me-and-I'll-do-likewise-for-you, a few odd thousands are seldom permitted to smash friendship.

So the committee went ahead with its investigation, rolling up bills for the taxpayers to pay in excess of the $25,000 to which it had been restricted by the Senate. The count continued, as everyone knows, long after the $25,000 was spent; the committee functioned for months when there was not so much as a thin dime to its credit. The $25,000 restriction, so far as the taxpayers were concerned, was meaningless to the committee. It might just as well have been omitted.

To complete the chapter of the committee's activity it is necessary to step out of the fiscal year by which this chronicle otherwise is bounded. Omitting the account of tedious months of counting and canvassing the ballots after the $25,000 had been spent, we come to the next session of Congress meeting December 7, 1931.

Three days after Congress convened, Shortridge of California, chairman of the full Committee on Privileges and Elections, submitted a resolution (Senate Resolution 69) asking the Senate to authorize the spending of $30,000 additional to defray the sub-committee's expenses. Seven days later the resolution was favorably reported by the Committee to Audit and Control the Contingent Expenses of the Senate. On that date, December 17, the resolution was adopted without objection.

Thus on December 17 the Hastings committee was authorized to exceed its limit of $25,000. It was the first time the committee had been authorized to exceed the $25,000 limit. Months after the debt had been incurred, the committee was authorized to incur it, to the extent of $30,000 more.

The $30,000, having been obligated in greater part or in full before it was authorized, didn't last long. Within a month, the committee was back again for more. This time, January 15, 1932, it asked (Senate Resolution 139) for another $5,000. In six days it got the money. Thus the $25,000 investigation had grown to a $60,000 investigation.

But even that was not enough. On March 9, Senator Hastings introduced a resolution (Senate Resolution 185) authorizing $5,000 more. It was referred to the Committee to Audit and Control the Contingent Expenses of the Senate. The latter committee, apparently, was becoming fed up on the growing expense account of the Bankhead-Heflin contest, and this time it took no action. Twelve days passed and not a nickel more was forthcoming. Then there was introduced another resolution (Senate Resolution 188) asking for $1,142.76 to pay witnesses. And still the Audit and Control committee kept the till closed.

Senator Hastings waited eleven days more. Then he introduced still another resolution (Senate Resolution 189) asking for $5,000. The investigating committee really needed the money, but the Audit and Control committee, like the owl that lived in the oak, said nothing. And the Hastings committee got what the owl said.

Meantime, the investigation was practically ended. In the last days of April the genial Mr. Heflin played his one remaining card. He sensed, apparently, that the decision was against him, so he craved the permission of his former "fellow Senators" to present his own case before them. This strange and unusual request was considered and Mr. Heflin was accorded the boon he sought. History holds no parallel for his five-hour harangue on the floor of the Senate in those closing days of April, 1932. Merely to print the long address in the *Congressional Record,* at about $40 a page, cost the taxpayers approximately $1,134. As a private citizen Mr. Heflin poured out his heart, but his plea was denied. Bankhead, as everyone knows, was voted the seat.

And now the case had been finally and definitely disposed of by the Senate itself. What chance would the sub-committee have now to obtain authority for spending more money? Indeed, what need did the committee have to spend? The case was decided; the chapter had been ended; finis had been written.

Yet on May 11, two weeks after Heflin's claims had been rejected, Senator Hastings introduced still another resolution (Senate Resolution 213) asking that the Senate authorize his committee to spend $35,000 more on the Bankhead-Heflin investigation. Of such farcical stuff is some legislation. The investigation had been ended nearly a fortnight before, yet here was a request for authority to spend $35,000 more. Why?

The reason must appear clear: authority to spend was sought because the committee already had incurred the obligation. It was not to be a fresh spending on a subject already disposed of, but a legalizing of spendings already obligated without authority of law. Just that; for if such spendings had been authorized, why was authority now sought? No; the committee had obligated itself for the money, every dollar, doubtless, notwithstanding that provision of the law which limits spendings to the amounts appropriated.

The day after this resolution was introduced, it won the approval of the Audit and Control committee, but the sum was cut from $35,000 to $30,000. And two days later, on May 14, the resolution was adopted, after some discussion, by the Senate. On that date the Hastings committee was given authority to incur and pay a debt of $30,000 on a case disposed of in the preceding month. In other words, the Senate obligingly saved the committee's face and put its O. K. on debts the committee had contracted.

By those steps, notwithstanding the plain language of the law, a $25,000 investigation was turned into a $90,000 investigation. Ninety thousand dollars is what the Bankhead-Heflin controversy cost the federal taxpayers.

What does the law amount to in such a case? Nothing; it is as dead as King Tut. The Senate said $25,000; the committee said $90,000; and the taxpayers said, "Here it is." Why bother with laws if the lawmakers themselves shamelessly may flaunt them?

Theoretically that law is observed, because the actual spendings are not made; practically it is disregarded because commitments are made in discount of future favorable action by the Senate. The taxpayers receive from this law about as much protection as one would receive from a coverless umbrella during a downpour. Senatorial courtesy demands that the reasonable commitments of investigating Senators be upheld, notwithstanding the intent of the law.

Further, the law has no penalty. It carries no punishment for those who break it. The law simply says don't and there it stops. If it were given teeth, if it carried a penalty clause that inflicted removal from office upon offenders, it would be observed. If it were clarified to include commitments, direct or indirect, as well as actual spendings, it would be impossible to charge the taxpayers $90,000 for an investigation limited to $25,000 as was done in this case.

Chapter VIII

Sherlock on the Job at $128,000 a Year

"I can see," said Senator Nye, "these pages from the *Congressional Record* in the pocket of every political foe in North Dakota next year when I shall be seeking re-election.

"I can hear tongues wagging and I can see lips moving in whispers, pointing out some little item in this account showing how lavishly Nye lives when he is out on government expense, showing how liberally he tips when he is out on government expense, showing what extraordinary and lavish accommodations he insists on having at hotels when he is out on government expense. Look at this item—a meal costing $12 or some such sum—and I know what the result will be."

So spoke the Senator from North Dakota to his colleagues in the Senate chamber on January 29, 1931. Wearied yet pressing on, he was nearing the end of a long, cold trail. For nine months he and his pack had yapped at the heels of campaign scandal. The chase lay through many States, and many keen-nosed experts had bayed down many a back-track. Far and wide they had followed the scent of campaign dollars spent in the 1930 senatorial elections. With first $100,000 from the treasury and then with $50,000 more, the Nye committee had policed, as best it could, both primaries and the general election. But real scandal, if such there were, had eluded them.

Lately he had stood before the Senate where he stood now, his $100,000 gone, asking for more. As the creature of the august body he addressed he had told the Senators that to continue the task he would require more money. Even as he spoke, he said, a score of witnesses were ready to start from Pennsylvania for a hearing before his committee at Washington, but the money to pay their traveling expenses and fees was not available. His fund was exhausted. His request for more had met with no action. Unless more money were forthcoming within the day, the witnesses would be notified to stay at home and the investigation would end.

Hurriedly, they had voted him $50,000 more. The Committee on Audit and Control, voting the funds, had exacted his promise, however, that he would submit within three days a full accounting for what already had been spent. The three days had passed. Three more, three more, and yet three more had come and gone and still the accounting was delayed. Finally, thirteen days after the $50,000 had been voted, Senator Moses, President pro tem, had got the documents from the disbursing clerk and obtained the Senate's permission to have them printed in the *Congressional Record*. They covered many pages.

Senator Nye's prophecy was uttered with those pages in mind. His expense account was spread on the record. How could he explain it to the folks back home? Would they not believe he alone had spent that money? Would they consider how, why and where the money had been spent? Or would they simply point him out as the man who spent—or said he spent—$100,000 in nine months? Those printed pages in the *Congressional Record,* he feared, would cost him dear in 1932.

Senator Nye and his four colleagues on the committee did, indeed, spend $100,000. To be exact, they spent $128,795.69 in the fiscal year 1931 alone. They spent some more in 1930 and some more in 1932. All told, their expenses probably touched the $150,000 appropriated for them. The final accounting has not been published as this is written. Their spendings averaged $10,700 a month during the year; for a time they exceeded $15,000 a month. As an instance of generous spendings, the Nye committee is monumental, and like a great many other Senate committees, it brought home a minimum of bacon for a maximum of effort.

But for what was spent and what was accomplished, Senator Nye and his colleagues are accountable only as agents. The stunt was not their idea. It did not originate with any of them. None of them desired the rather disagreeable assignment. Nye was asked and consented to take the chairmanship after other Senators had declined to serve. His committee served the Senate capably in a bit of a wildgoose chase, but they did not originate the chase itself.

On the Senate lies full responsibility for the $150,000 spending. Whatever wasting of the taxpayers' funds there may have been in those depression years was the Senate's wasting, not Nye's. Senator Nye cannot be charged properly with the extravagance; it rests on the Senate's doorstep.

The spending starting with the adoption by the Senate on April 10, 1930, of a resolution authorizing the Vice-President to appoint a committee to go through the country and ferret out the moneys spent by senatorial candidates during the election of 1930. The Smith-Vare spendings in the 1926 campaigns in Illinois and Pennsylvania were of recent memory. Two sentiments seem to have welled up in senatorial breasts; one, that such heavy expenditures should be curbed; the other, that the facts concerning all campaign spendings by senatorial candidates should be surveyed.

Without dissent, the Senate adopted the resolution providing a senatorial survey of such spendings. With the resolution went an appropriation of $100,000. The depression had not yet fastened its fangs deeply upon the American economic structure. Gauged by the mammoth appropriation for government departments, $100,000 was more or less small change. So, offhand, it was appropriated.

The need for the spending does not seem so clearly defined in some lay minds as in the opinion of the Senators authorizing it. There was on the statute books then the same corrupt practices Act as now. The Department of Justice then was as fully empowered as now to seek and punish violators. The same penitentiary would welcome the guilty convicted by the Department as that welcoming the guilty shown up by the Senate. In short, the $150,000 spending appears to have been a duplication by the Senate, certainly in its purpose, of work provided for in the budget of the Attorney General. Nevertheless, the Senate decided that it should investigate. It probably would have reached the same decision had the cost of the investigation been $500,000 or $1,000,000. So it went ahead. It would have the facts from its own garnering should another heavy spender seek admission to the Senate.

Nye's associates were Dale of Vermont, Dill of Washington, Wagner of New York and Patterson of Missouri. Occasionally their names bob up in the record of spendings, but for the most part the work was directed by their chairman.

The work was well under way when the fiscal year 1931 started, on July 1. By that time Nye had the country blocked off by districts and investigators had been assigned to cover various sections. As election day approached, the committee's work speeded up and its forces increased. In October, 1930, just before election, there were fourteen investigators out in the field, gathering data. With two exceptions, the investigators received salaries of $500 a month apiece. One of the fourteen received $250 a month and another $275.

The fourteen investigators swung the total pay roll for the field effort to $6,525 in October. The secretary of the committee received $500 a month, too, and there were clerks at Washington in addition. The expenses of the investigators were not small. Here is the way they appear, during October, on the record:

P. L. Aarhus, covering Nebraska and Illinois, expenses from October 5 to November 1, inclusive, $249.49.

W. Hunter Baldwin, covering Illinois and Tennessee, expenses from October 5 to November 1, inclusive, $276.95.

Charles C. Barnard, covering Tennessee, expenses from October 7 to 27, inclusive, $194.39.

F. H. Creech, covering Nebraska, expenses from October 9 to 27, inclusive, $185.25.

E. M. Daniel, covering Illinois and Tennessee, expenses from October 5 to November 1, inclusive, $274.26.

Frank E. Healy, covering Nebraska, expenses from October 5 to 25, $221.21.

H. J. Loose, in Illinois, expenses during September, $13.26.

Bernard D. Reed, covering Delaware, expenses during October, $75.

P. D. Norton, expenses in Montana, October 11 to November 1, inclusive, $255.15.

Howard M. Rice, covering Delaware, expenses from October 8 to 23, inclusive, $135.77.

Western Starr, covering Massachusetts, expenses from October 7 to November 3 (including $50 automobile hire for Senator Wagner, a member of the committee), $194.45.

J. L. Ward, covering North Carolina, expenses from October 4 to 19, $310.26.

Russell M. McFarland, covering Pennsylvania, expenses from October 27 to November 2, $97.15.

Ingham C. Mack, covering West Virginia, expenses from September 30 to October 29, $347.01.

For the fourteen investigators in the field, traveling, subsistence, hotel bills and other expenses, listed above, totaled $2,829.40. Roughly, the period covered is the month of October. When the $6,525 paid the investigators in salaries is added to their expense accounts the total runs to $9,404.40. For field investigation, it thus appears, the taxpayers were charged at the rate of nearly $113,000 a year.

This rate of spending, quickening somewhat as election neared, had continued at approximately that level for months. The investigators interviewed thousands of private citizens, including, in many cases, the candidates themselves. Almost every enemy of every candidate, Republican or Democratic, lent his voice, at some time during the campaign, to an investigator's ear. It probably was the greatest political snooping stunt ever staged in the United States or any other country.

In Massachusetts, for instance, Conrad Crooker, helping in the fight on a Republican candidate, called for a Senate committee investigator to come to the State. Senator Nye sent a capable man, rejoicing in the name of Western Starr, who stayed four weeks at Boston (at a cost of about $600 to the treasury) but found no violation of the law. That instance was on a par with scores of others. Later Mr. Crooker came to Washington (at the treasury's expense) and served the committee two days (at $10 a day) and went home, but nothing came of the committee's investigation in Massachusetts. At least, nothing showing the violation of the law or warranting Senate action.

All over the United States, in every State where the contest was hard-fought, the same sort of thing happened. For a time the committee was spending nearly $500 a day following leads, holding hearings, dispatching its detectives here, there and yonder, and finding precious little in the way of law violation, though swarms of witnesses poured their stories into senatorial ears. Once started by the somewhat reluctant Nye, the search for the mare's nest continued with bigger and better spendings.

For a time, Senator Nye's brother, Donald, was in charge of the committee's spendings. Donald O. Nye appears on the Senate pay roll as an assistant clerk to the Committee on Public Lands and Surveys at $2,880 a year. The Senator obviously borrowed him from that committee to meet the need for capability, loyalty and integrity essential to the job. This $55-a-week employee supervised the committee's big spendings for months, handling the cash for his brother. While few Senate committees have spent money faster, it is the opinion of the Senate's disbursing officials that few committees, if any, have ever had a more capable accounting rendered of their spendings.

Some of Donald Nye's bills, for sheer size, made even the experienced pay-off men in the Senate's disbursing office look twice. On October 15, for instance, Mr. Nye presented a bill for $7,925.20. It covered part of the committee's expenses during the preceding thirty days. On November 7 he was back with another bill for $6,752.74. Even those bills did not represent the full head of steam under which the committee was spending money. Many other items of smaller dimensions were paid direct.

Mr. Nye's expense accounts show that his brother, the Senator, was not the only member of the committee out in the field, working and spending, during that period. Some of the highlights of his bill of October 15 (which included all the expenses of the fourteen investigators for the preceding month) are as follows:

> Paid to Palmer House, Chicago, for accommodations of Senators Nye, Dale and Wagner and assistants for period of September 14 to 20, $497.01.
> Paid in advance to D. H. McArthur and John Andrews on August 6, for expenses for investigation in

Tennessee, Oklahoma, Illinois, and Minnesota, $1,000.

Paid to Baltimore & Ohio Railroad Company for transportation and pullman charges for Senator Nye and assistants from Washington, D. C. to Chicago and St. Paul, September 13-15, $293.24.

Paid to Chicago, Burlington & Quincy Railroad Company for transportation and pullman charges for Senators Nye and Dale and assistants from Lincoln to Chicago, to Omaha and to Washington, D. C., September 25, $249.28.

Paid to Hotel Cornhusker, Lincoln, Neb., for accommodations for Senators Nye and Dale and assistants for period from September 21 to 25, $295.35.

Paid to witnesses (eleven were named) for witness fees and expenses in Nebraska hearings September 21 to 25, $286.31.

Paid to Senator Patterson for reimbursement of expenses in attending hearing in Chicago, September 14 to 17—

Transportation, including pullman charges, Kansas City to Chicago and return	$ 58.64
Hotel accommodations at Chicago	18.00
Subsistence en route and at Chicago	30.00
Taxi fares and porterage	5.35
Total paid Senator Patterson	$111.99

Paid to Senator Dill for reimbursement of expenses in attending hearing at Chicago, Sept. 14-20—

Transportation, including pullman charges, Spokane to Chicago and return	$375.28
Subsistence en route and at Chicago	43.96
Taxi fares and porterage	1.85
Total paid Senator Dill	$421.09

Paid to Senator Wagner for reimbursement of expenses in attending hearing at Chicago, September 14 to 18—
Transportation, including pullman charges,
   New York to Chicago and return........$142.26
Subsistence en route 2.50
                                  _____

    Total paid Senator Wagner $144.76

From these listings, so far as Messrs. Patterson, Dill and Wagner are concerned, it is seen that the spendings for railroad and pullman fares are considerably in excess of the published charges for transportation and lower berth. Probably the three Senators occupied pullman compartments or drawing rooms.

Chairman Nye himself submitted on October 9 a bill for $1,412.20 covering expenses from August 6 to September 30. During that period the Senator spent much time traveling, and his bill includes items paid out on behalf of his fellow members and assistants. The grouping of transportation charges, including pullman charges, meals en route and porterage, runs to $889.33. A part of this was incurred for Senators Dale, Wagner and Dill, traveling with him from Belton, Montana, to Fargo; and elsewhere transportation was bought for Senator Nye's clerk or assistant. That, too, was in the bill. Subsistence at various hotels during the period amounted to $161.70. Some of this was paid for other members of the committee and employees. Hotel accommodations at Fargo and Chicago were listed at $79.43, including meals at Fargo; other expenses made up a total of $282.74 additional.

Donald Nye's $6,752.74 expense account of November 7 shows the speed of investigation during October. It contains, as usual, the expenses of the corps of $500-a-month investigators, other items including the following:

Paid to Battery Park Hotel, Asheville, N. C., for accommodations for Senator Patterson and assistants on Oct. 14 (including transportation Asheville to Washington) $69.13.

Paid to Senator R. C. Patterson for reimbursement of expenses for himself and assistant incurred in attending hearings in North Carolina, Oct. 7 to 14, inclusive, as follows:

Transportation, including pullman charges,
Kansas City to Washington, D. C., and
return $115.90
St. Louis to Washington, D. C., and return.. 83.08
Asheville, N. C. to Washington, D. C. 45.48
Hotel accommodations and subsistence..... 75.25
Taxi fares and porterage 46.50

Total paid Senator Patterson $366.21

Paid to Sir Walter Hotel, Raleigh, N. C., for accommodations for Senators Nye, Patterson, Wagner and assistants, on Oct. 12 and 13, $90.80.

Paid to Andrew Jackson Hotel, Nashville, Tenn., for accommodations for Senators Nye and Wagner and assistants, from Oct. 12 to 16, $114.25.

Paid to Hotel Peabody, Memphis, Tenn., for accommodations for Senators Nye and Wagner and assistants, Oct. 17 to 20, $264.92.

Paid to Peabody ticket office, Memphis, Tenn., for transportation, including pullman charges for Senators Nye and Wagner and assistants, to New York, Washington, and Omaha, $240.13.

And so the bills accumulated. The investigators, working well and faithfully, presented modest bills. Covering the better part of the United States, however, costs money. The taxpayers paid the bills. Nor were expenses afield the only bills to come rolling into the treasury. Early in the fiscal year Senator Nye availed himself of the services of an expert accountant, Lloyd E. Bemis, whose bill, paid August 20, is as follows:

For services as accountant, and for services of assistants, in the investigation of contributions and expenditures of senatorial candidates, under resolution of April 10, 1930, as follows:
During month of July—

12 days at $40	$480.00
13 days at $25	325.00
5 days at $25	125.00
Expenses (taxi and carfare)	8.04
Total	$938.04

In June the committee had employed Mr. Bemis, paying him $1,034.40. In August Mr. Bemis' services and those of his assistants, at the same rates of pay, totaled $305.

They also incurred expenses amounting to $106.55. In September the Bemis services and those of his assistants amounted to $710. Thereafter, the Nye committee appears to have conducted its affairs without benefit of experts (other than its $500-a-month investigators) until February, 1931. In that month, Basil M. Manly became attached to the committee as a special assistant. The election then was three months in the back calendar. Within less than a month the newly elected Senators would enter upon their terms. The Nye committee still labored, however, with its investigation.

As related in a preceding chapter, Mr. Manly first appeared in Senate Document No. 1 (the Report of the Secretary of the Senate for the fiscal year 1931) as a $50-a-day expert employed by the Capper committee investigating the reasons why bread was not selling for five cents a loaf. Mr. Manly had worked for ten days, including Sundays, for the Capper committee, his employment ending February 7. He then took a day off. On February 9 he reappeared on the pay roll as a $40-a-day "special assistant" of the Nye committee. From that time until the ending of the fiscal year he remained on the Nye committee pay roll, receiving the following sums for his services:

> February services, 18 days ....$ 720
> March services, 24 days 960
> April services, 26 days 1,040

May services, 26 days 1,040
June services, 15 days 600

During the five months, Mr. Manly served 109 days and received $4,360 compensation. Seven months after the election was over, he was still serving as a special assistant at $40 a day.

Mr. Manly was not the only person, however, who found lucrative pickings in the Nye committee service. The record shows that the stenographers who reported the various hearings held by the committee were enriched to the extent of $3,591.84 (and that does not include some of the minor hearings) as follows:

William M. Day, 5 days' hearings, July and
    August $1,232.98
William M. Day, 4 days' hearings, Sep-
    tember 616.00
Satterlee, Binns & Boos, 2 days' hearings,
    September 196.00
Sidney M. Smith, 2 days' hearings, October.. 266.90
Clara Mason, 1 day's hearing, August 24.30
William M. Day, 10 days' hearings, Septem-
    ber and October 1,255.66
William M. Day, 5 days' hearings, November
    and December 723.76
William M. Day, 9 days' hearings, November
    and December 1,488.28
William M. Day, 10 days' hearings, January.. 1,146.60
William M. Day, 2 days' hearings, February 498.52
William M. Day, 3 days' hearings, May..... 344.85

For these services and other expenses, the committee's spendings during the fiscal year, according to Senate Document No. 1, ran to a total of $57,471.86.

For salaries paid the fourteen investigators, Mr. Manly, Mr. Bemis, clerks, stenographers and other employees during the fiscal year, the committee's spendings totaled $71,323.83.

Between July 1, 1930, and June 30, 1931, the Nye committee spent, for all purposes, $128,795.69.

In June, 1931, seven months after the election had been held, the committee turned in the following bills to the treasury:

> June 4. F. H. Creech, expenses as investigator from May 24 to 30 ....$ 87.01
> June 4. Charles Hanratty, serving subpoenas in October, 1930 .... 4.52
> June 10. P. L. Aarhus, expenses as investigator from May 24 to May 30 .... 145.50
> June 10. F. H. Creech, expenses as investigator from May 31 to June 6 .... 111.37
> June 10. Edward M. Daniel, expenses as investigator from May 29 to June 5 .... 86.65
> June 12. Chesapeake & Potomac Telephone Company, long distance calls, Nov. 1 to Feb. 14 28.35
> June 18. F. H. Creech, salary, June 1-15, inclusive 250.00
> June 18. F. H. Creech, expenses as investigator from June 7 to 13 .... 150.68
> June 18. Edward M. Daniel, expenses as investigator, June 7 to 13 .... 94.46

June 18. Advance on expenses, Washington to points in Nebraska and Oklahoma and return 250.00

June 24. P. D. Norton, expenses as investigator from May 24 to 30 .... 123.46

June 24. W. Hunter Baldwin, expenses as investigator, June 1 to 9 .... 93.77

June 30. John Andrews, June salary as secretary 500.00

June 30. W. Hunter Baldwin, June salary as investigator 500.00

June 30. Edward M. Daniel, June salary as investigator 500.00

June 30. J. E. Johnson, June salary as assistant clerk 200.00

June 30. Catherine Ladwig, June salary as assistant clerk 200.00

June 30. Basil M. Manly, special assistant, 15 days' services in June at $40 .... 600.00

June 30. Agnes M. Rydgren, June salary as assistant clerk 150.00

June 30. F. H. Creech, salary, June 16-30.... 250.00

June 30. Elizabeth Winslow, June services as typist and clerk 100.00

June 30. Edward M. Daniel, expenses as investigator, June 15 to 27 .... 125.62

Such was the picture: total spendings of $4,551.39 during a month, more than half a year after the election; three investigators at $500 a month apiece, a secretary at $500, a special assistant at $600, and four clerks at $550 for the four; a total pay roll of $3,150—somewhat better than $100 a day. Somebody might have tipped off the committee that the election was over, that everybody except themselves had gone home.

But no; these investigations hang on like a summer cold. Originally sponsored to end in December, 1930, the investigation was extended to the first legislative day in January, 1932. Originally estimated to cost $100,000 it ended with appropriations of $150,000.

Who benefited? The railroads; they deposited many thousands in their tills in fares paid by the committee and its investigators. The hotels; their bills bespatter the expense account like big drops of rain in a sudden summer shower. The process servers; their fees are strung through the spendings. The witnesses—maybe; they came in squads with the treasury paying their way and their fees. The fourteen investigators; they got $500 a month apiece in a dull time when jobs were scarce. The committee itself; it lived at least a part of the time on its expense account. The stenographers; reporting jobs paying up to $1,400 for a few days' hearings were scarcer than hen's teeth those days.

How about the taxpayers? Is it possible that the men and women who paid the mammoth bills failed to benefit, too? What have they to show for the vanished thousands?

It is quite likely that the taxpayers' benefits cannot be measured. It is quite likely that the moral effect of the committee served to prevent huge campaign spendings, though that is debatable. It is quite likely that the Senate, of whose personnel one-third was elected in 1930, is a purer, better, nobler Senate than it would be today had not the Nye committee stood, like a valiant policeman, at the crossing.

Anyhow, the taxpayers' $150,000 was spent and the Senators were elected. It was another noble experiment. Charge it off; thus:

To improving the Senate's quality, $150,000.

Chapter IX

Hot Air, Petty Graft and Merry Christmas

Talk is cheap. But not in Congress. The price tag on Senate chatter in 1931 was approximately $90,000. For reporting the debates in the Senate the treasury paid $60,340. For reporting the hearings before Senate committees, which spawned to the number of 134 during the year, the cost was $28,292.02. That was the beginning. Printing and circulating the Babel of words followed.

Official stenographers of the Senate receive about $5,000 a month under an arrangement going back to 1919. They earn it. Whether the Senate is in long adjournment or continuous session, the amount is the same. When the Senate is in session, the official stenographers probably lose money. The holidays, when there is no work, compensate for the loss. Their profits, if any, are made during those months.

Official stenographers do not cover Senate committee hearings. Private firms of stenographic experts, in the main resident in Washington, attend to that. Each committee hires shorthand experts to cover its hearings. The experts are paid 25 cents per 100 words of testimony, upon delivery of the original transcript. If more than one copy is wanted, the shorthand men are paid five cents per 100 words for each carbon copy. Often five carbon copies are purchased; sometimes six.

The rate is regarded as fair. With allowance for idle time during a hearing, the experts record about 100 words per minute. An hour's hearing, at that average, would produce 6,000 words of testimony. For taking that down in shorthand and transcribing it, the expert would receive $15. If five carbon copies are bought, he receives $30. His gross earnings, however, cannot be estimated at $30 for the hour, as considerable time is necessary for transcribing.

Approximately a dozen firms shared the Senate's $28,000 patronage (for committee hearings) in 1931. A few skimmed the cream. Hearings were held in great number, but the Nye committee, the Blaine committee, the Indian Affairs committee, the appropriations committee and a few others provided the bulk of the work. A wealth of words came in driblets from other committee hearings, apparently held without regard to cost and covering such subjects as:

Repurchase of the Vollbehr collection of incunabula.
Drought relief and unemployment.
Control of predatory animals.
Conservation of rainfall.

Outdoor signs.
Regulating the practice of the healing art.
Regulation of naturopathy.
Equal rights.
Trading on margins.
Birth control.
The preservation and improvement of Niagara
  Falls.
The halibut fishery.
International load line conventions.
The second polar year.
Closing Washington's barber shops on Sundays.
To make July 5 a legal holiday.
Vivisection.

Those, in the main, were minor hearings. They are
instances of fattening the Senate's spendings. They are
paid out of federal taxes.

Like speeches delivered on the Senate floor, these hearings often are printed and distributed fairly widely under
frank through the mails. Not to the extent, however, of
the speeches of Senators. House and Senate maintain
forces to fold printed copies of speeches delivered by members and to mail them. Folders are paid one dollar for
folding 1,000 copies of a speech. In 1931 the Senate spent
$12,500 that way. At $1 per 1,000, the expenditure discloses that 12,500,000 copies of speeches were folded, to be
franked through the mails at taxpayers' expense. The

House spent $13,854. That means the distribution, under frank, of 13,854,000 copies of addresses delivered in the House. Thus more than 26,000,000 copies of speeches delivered in Congress in 1931 were franked through the mails—probably a trainload of printed matter—at a cost of $26,354 for folding alone.

Post Office Department officials estimate that postage for matter franked through the Washington post office during the year would cost about $3,000,000. Arbitrarily, a sum approximating $3,000,000 was placed in 1931 to the credit of the Washington post office in order that its volume of clearings might take proper rank with those of other post offices throughout the country. Included in franked mail, however, were the mailings of the various executive departments as well as those of House and Senate. How much of the $3,000,000 represents matter mailed by Congress is undetermined.

Whatever the sum—and it was large— it was but a fraction of the total cost to the country of the 1931 crop of hot air in Congress. To figures already given should be added printing costs, labor and materials. Stationery alone ran to hundreds of thousands, perhaps millions, of dollars. In providing stationery, the taxpayers apparently have been forgotten altogether. A few sheets of paper cost little or nothing; tons of paper, purchased in carload lots, run into money. In buying paper, House and Senate apparently think of the cost of the few sheets, rather than the carloads.

The lack of respect for the taxpayers' rights is disclosed by the petty grafting in stationery by members of both Houses. Take the Senate, for instance.

Every Senator starts the fiscal year with an allowance of $125 for stationery. For that sum, it is estimated, he may purchase all the letterheads, envelopes, carbon paper, typewriter ribbons, notebooks and pencils necessary to conduct his official correspondence during the year. To provide the Senators with these and similar supplies an official stationery shop is maintained in the Senate Office Building. If he wishes, a Senator may pay cash for his stationery.

Senate committees likewise are furnished stationery by the official shop but no limit of $125 a year is imposed on the committees. Every member of the Senate is a member of one or more committees. His membership gives him the privilege of using committee stationery.

Under that arrangement a thrifty Senator, scorning not the nickels and dimes flowing into his private pocketbook, may obtain much, if not all, of the stationery he requires through his committee. Many, probably the majority, of the Senators do just that thing. The result is that the personal allotment of $125 a year per Senator for stationery is seldom checked out in full at the official stationery shop. There generally is a credit, owing to the Senator. For that credit he may take either stationery or cash.

He takes the cash. Here is what the various Senators received in cash at the close of the fiscal year 1931, representing in each case, the difference between the amount charged against them for stationery during the year and the $125 allotted them:

Ashurst of Arizona ....$ 24.10
Bingham of Connecticut 10.67
Black of Alabama 62.88
Blaine of Wisconsin 72.58
Borah of Idaho 90.54
Brookhart of Iowa 19.62
Broussard of Louisiana 80.96
Capper of Kansas 117.42
Caraway of Arkansas 32.76
Connally of Texas 26.85
Cutting of New Mexico 40.74
Dill of Washington 15.42
Fess of Ohio 51.92
Fletcher of Florida 43.61
Frazier of Minnesota 92.36
George of Georgia 47.03
Goldsborough of Maryland 41.33
Harris of Georgia 45.32
Hastings of Delaware 77.25
Hayden of Arizona 14.04
Howell of Nebraska 88.17
Johnson of California 94.86
Jones of Washington 63.53
Kendrick of Wyoming 85.41

Keyes of New Hampshire 107.29
King of Utah 7.63
McNary of Oregon 113.48
Moses of New Hampshire 112.40
Norris of Nebraska 108.10
Reed of Pennsylvania 71.50
Robinson of Arkansas 90.80
Robinson of Indiana 10.69
Sheppard of Texas 125.00
Smith of South Carolina 32.74
Smoot of Utah 54.77
Steiwer of Oregon 50.37
Stephens of Mississippi 67.51
Swanson of Virginia 30.47
Thomas of Idaho 18.82
Thomas of Oklahoma 125.00
Townsend of Delaware 75.27
Trammell of Florida 98.55
Tydings of Maryland 68.56
Vandenberg of Michigan 23.51
Walcott of Connecticut 17.35
Walsh of Massachusetts 12.58
Walsh of Montana 31.56
Waterman of Colorado 80.49
Watson of Indiana 45.04

The fiscal year 1931 was marked by the passage from
public life of certain Senators whose terms of office ended

March 4. In those cases the Senators were credited with their proportionate part of the $125 allowance for the year, starting with July 1 and ending March 3, or about $83.50 for each Senator. On March 3, the day before their retirement, the disbursing officer ascertained how much stationery each of those Senators had withdrawn on his account and sent him a check for the remainder of the $83.50, as follows:

Brock of Tennessee	$ 31.38
Deneen of Illinois	15.04
Gillett of Massachusetts	40.54
Goff of West Virginia	19.99
Gould of Maine	22.56
Heflin of Alabama	24.73
McMaster of South Dakota	22.41
Pine of Oklahoma	54.14
Simmons of North Carolina	27.45

During the year two Senators died—Overman of North Carolina on December 12, and Greene of Vermont on December 17. The commutation of allowance for stationery was figured by the disbursing officer in the case of each of those Senators and checks forwarded the proper persons for $27.22 and $54.42, respectively.

Sixty Senators, as cited above, are named in the Secretary's Report. The amount paid them in cash totaled $3,258.73. Their combined stationery allowance was about $7,200. Instead of turning back to the treasury the

excess of their allowances, these Senators took the money
—about two-fifths of the total allowance—and stuck it
into their pockets. It represented their personal profit on
stationery, at the taxpayers' expense, during the year.

Was it legal? Yes; the Senators had a legal right to do
it. It is not only legal but customary. Two generations
or so of Senators have done it. So if custom can purify,
the practice is pure. But the question still persists—what
did the taxpayers get in return for the $3,258.73 that the
Senators crammed into their private pockets? And it
answers itself; the taxpayers got nothing. Nothing except the bill, which they paid, as usual. The record discloses nothing more.

This legalized petty grafting by Senators, small and
sorry though it be, is not the whole of the sordid story.
The official stationery shop carries many things on its
shelves. These it purchases at wholesale prices and sells
at cost. Fountain pens and desk sets, for instance, are
bought at from 43 to 45 percent discount from the retail
prices fetched in private stationery stores. Brief cases and
other kindred supplies are available to Senators at far
less than the usual retail prices.

The record for 1931 shows that the official stationery
shop did a flourishing business in fountain pens and desk
sets. Scores were sold, at somewhat more than one-half
of what they would have sold for in any of Washington's
stores. A Senator wanting a fine fountain pen need only
step into the stationery shop, or send his clerk. The

Senator could get what he wanted at about half price. Moreover, out of his $125 allowance the bill would be paid—by the taxpayers. The government thus would present the Senator with the pen.

Scores, perhaps, hundreds of fountain pens were repaired at nominal cost through the stationery shop. Whether these repairs extended to the pens of the Senator's clerks is not disclosed. The number sold and the number repaired seem incredibly large for the personal needs of the ninety-six Senators alone.

The official stationery shop carried an attractive line of Christmas cards, as well. These were available to the ninety-six Senators. Senator Blank, wishing to gladden his friends back home with holiday greetings, was able to do so merely for the postage. The Stationery shop was there to supply the cards (at considerably less than retail prices elsewhere) and the government was there to pay for the cards out of his $125 allowance. The allowance covered anything, within its limit, that the Senator might wish to purchase through the official shop.

More than 5,000 Christmas cards, the record shows, cleared through the official stationery shop in December, 1930. The taxpayers appear to have paid for every one. Every card was available, without cost, to the ninety-six Senators, up to a limit of $125. Where engraved Christmas cards were desired, from personally owned plates, the official shop attended to the engraving. Here are some of the entries from the official record:

Dec. 9. 1,000 No. 504 Christmas cards from die, Mr. and Mrs. Robinson, $60.

Dec. 9. 75 No. 547 Christmas cards from plate, Mr. and Mrs. George Compton, $5.50.

Dec. 9. 100 No. 538 Christmas cards from plate, Neva Butler, $7.25.

Dec. 9. 50 No. 52B28 Christmas cards from plate, Harriet Bentley, $4.00.

Dec. 9. 100 No. 519 Christmas cards from plate, Loveland, $7.25.

Dec. 11. 1 No. 4 line S.O.E. greeting plate, 1-plate arrangement: To imprinting 400 greeting cards and 1,500 special cards, $53.75.

Dec. 22. 25 No. 120 Christmas cards, $3.25.
Stamped Katheryn Robinson, $1.50.

Dec. 22. 100 No. 208 Christmas cards, $2.50.
Stamped Dora Lee Chaney, $2.25.

There are two Robinsons in the Senate. George O. Compton appears on the pay roll as clerk to the Committee on Pensions of which Senator Robinson of Indiana is chairman. Neva Butler is on the pay roll as assistant clerk to the Committee on Pensions, as is Harriet Bentley. Ailene J. Loveland likewise is assistant clerk to the same committee. Neither Katheryn Robinson nor Dora Lee Chaney appeared on the pay roll of the Senate during the fiscal year.

A good deal of printing and engraving for the Senate stationery shop appears to have been done during December by a Washington department store, Woodward

& Lothrop. This store's bills for such work, as disclosed by the official record, follow:

October	$ 454.41
November	517.52
December	1,888.59
January	685.77

Probably the entire excess of $1,300 in the December bill went to kid the taxpayers along—to wish them Merry Christmas at their own expense. Only a Senator, or a Representative, can do it.

The Senate, as shown, proceeds with dignity and decorum to pocket this petty legalized graft. There is no rushing up to the disbursing officer in mid-term to snatch a twenty- or a hundred-dollar bill on stationery account. To bespatter the mid-year with such crumbs is beneath senatorial dignity; Senators wait till the year ends to take their pickings. Then they are quite gentlemanly and deliberate as they slip the unearned dollars into their wallets.

It isn't that way in the House. Not at all. The House is quick and impulsive, stirred by the blood of younger and hotter years. There are a good many bald spots in the House, too, but most of the members are he-men in the prime of life. For those and other reasons, the $125 allowance is pepped up on its way to privacy.

Some of the Representatives apparently make a beeline for the disbursing officer as soon as they leave Union

Station. They have been back home for months, drawing only their salaries. They have to find in advance the money necessary to bring them to Washington. They are hard up. The $125 stationery allowance looks good to them. One hundred and twenty-five dollars in cash is important money at the moment. So they line up, some of them on the first day of the session, at the disbursing officer's window and take turns toting away the legal graft while the toting is good.

What the House does is a bit outside the pale of this recital. All that has been told up to this point is documented by the Annual Report of the Secretary of the Senate for 1931. However, as the stationery allowance for Representatives is the same as that for Senators, a digression to cover the House practice may be excused. What happened to the stationery allowance in the House is taken from House Document No. 2, the Annual Report of the Clerk of the House of Representatives for the Fiscal Year 1931. It therefore is fully documented and is official.

The House Document shows that on December 2 (the first day of the session), 3, 4, and 6, 1930, the following members drew their full stationery allowance of $125 each in cash:

Henry W. Temple of Pennsylvania.
William F. Stevenson of South Carolina.
Fritz G. Lanham of Texas.
Cassius C. Dowell of Iowa.

W. W. Chalmers of Ohio.
W. P. Lambertson of Kansas.
John N. Sandlin of Louisiana.
Robert L. Doughton of North Carolina.
John N. Garner of Texas.
George Huddleston of Alabama.
James T. Igoe of Illinois.
James C. McLaughlin of Michigan.
James G. Strong of Kansas.
Henry W. Watson of Pennsylvania.
Richard S. Aldrich of Rhode Island.
J. Zack Spearing of Louisiana.
Hatton W. Sumners of Texas.

To this list of seventeen Representatives who took the cash and let the credit go should be added another list of fourteen members who took part cash and part stationery during the first days of the session. What they drew in stationery before getting around to the cashier was deducted, in each case, from the $125 allowance. What they got in cash from December 2 to 6, inclusive, is shown in the official record as follows:

Milton W. Shreve of Pennsylvania, $105.32.
William C. Lankford of Georgia, $95.40.
Burton L. French of Idaho, $117.46.
Charles H. Brand of Georgia, $111.05.
W. A. Ayres of Kansas, $107.25.
James W. Collier of Mississippi, $94.53.
Numa F. Montet of Louisiana, $118.05.
Addison T. Smith of Idaho, $103.56.
Henry B. Steagall of Alabama, $94.55.

Robert H. Clancy of Michigan, $121.92.
Conrad G. Selvig of Minnesota, $109.61.
Charles J. Thompson of Ohio, $111.91.
Charles A. Jonas of North Carolina, $57.85.
John H. Kerr of North Carolina, $88.75.

It wasn't exactly a stampede, but the cashier was fairly busy paying Representatives their stationery money during those four days. The 31 members who got theirs had a combined stationery credit, at $125 each, amounting to $3,875. The record shows that they took $312.79 worth of free stationery and $3,562.21 worth of free coin of the realm. The stationery they put in their offices; the money they put in their pockets. And that was that.

Christmas was coming along fast and times were hard. The cashier was to receive similar visits, prior to the holidays, from other members of the House. Here, according to the official record, is how they came and what they got, in cash, from their stationery funds:

December 9.

Guy E. Campbell of Pennsylvania, $100.63.
Thomas S. McMillan of South Carolina, $106.81.
Edward E. Denison of Illinois, $125.
Marvin Jones of Texas, $125.
Pearl P. Oldfield of Arkansas, $125.
Sam Rayburn of Texas, $125.

December 10.

Katherine Langley of Kentucky, $19.66.
Gale H. Stalker of New York, $125.

December 11.

Grant E. Mouser of Ohio, $67.66.
James O'Connor of Louisiana, $125.
Tilman B. Parks of Arkansas, $110.81.

December 12.

John C. Allen of Illinois, $125.
Charles G. Edwards of Georgia, $117.82.
J. Charles Linthicum of Maryland, $125.
M. Alfred Michaelson of Illinois, $125.

December 13.

James J. Connolly of Pennsylvania, $125.
Rene L. DeRouen of Louisiana, $122.80.
Stanley H. Kunz of Illinois, $94.64.
John M. Nelson of Wisconsin, $125.

December 15.

D. D. Glover of Arkansas, $125.
Edward M. Beers of Pennsylvania, $125.
Schuyler Otis Bland of Virginia, $125.
Jeff Busby of Mississippi, $116.78.
J. Mitchell Chase of Pennsylvania, $65.62.

December 16.

W. M. Whittington of Mississippi, $125.
Carl Vinson of Georgia, $125.
Charles R. Crisp of Georgia, $125.
Lindsay C. Warren of North Carolina, $96.56.

December 18.

Henry Allen Cooper of Wisconsin, $92.38.

December 19.

Morgan G. Sanders of Texas, $104.90.
Charles I. Sparks of Kansas, $125.
E. E. Cox of Georgia, $125.
Martin J. Kennedy of New York, $78.79.
Percy E. Quin of Mississippi, $94.
H. St. George Tucker of Virginia, $85.45.
William C. Wright of Georgia, $79.36.

December 20.

Don B. Colton of Utah, $109.07.
Riley J. Wilson of Louisiana, $125.
Franklin Menges of Pennsylvania, $125.
Harry C. Canfield of Indiana, $125.
John E. Rankin of Mississippi, $125.
Nathan L. Strong of Pennsylvania, $98.53.
Charles C. Kearns of Ohio, $125.

December 23.

Loring M. Black of New York, $114.44.

December 24.

Sam B. Hill of Washington, $125.
Jacob L. Milligan of Missouri, $87.09.

That's the way they do it in the House. Between the opening of the session and Christmas Day 77 members had dropped in at the cashier's office and drawn their $125 in cash, or so much of it as remained to their credit. In Appendix B to this volume, the full list of all payments is shown.

134

The Representatives who drew this money from the treasury and put it away in their pocketbooks probably didn't think about it the second time. Doubtless it never occurred to any of them that they were taking money from the taxpayers for which a return should be given. Doubtless it never entered the thoughts of one of these honorable men that the taxpayers here were wholly at their mercy, having no say as to the right or wrong of what they were doing. And doubtless every mother's son of them believed and still believes that he was doing a perfectly natural and honorable thing in taking this money. It had been done for years; the money was there for them; so why not get it?

But what did the taxpayers get for that money? Was it spent later during the session to provide the stationery which it was appropriated to provide? Did the Representatives spend that $125 apiece for supplies to be used in their official correspondence? Or did they tuck it away, to be spent in whole or in part for Christmas presents, and eke out on stationery they could get free of cost from their various committees?

These are pertinent questions. They go to the right and the wrong of this practice. They can be answered only by the Representatives who pocketed the money. Under their high privilege, no power can compel them to an accounting. Under the trust imposed in them by the American people who elected them and sent them to Washington, public funds were their especial concern.

Under their oath of office, they pledged themselves to uphold the Constitution of the United States—and the Constitution authorizes no graft.

Were they true to their trust? Or did they dishonor themselves and their constituencies by pocketing for their personal gain these petty, contemptible sums from the public purse whose integrity they had sworn to guard? They can make reply, each according to his ideas of truth and falsehood. They—and they alone.

Chapter X

Other Perquisites

A drink of water for the Senator, many times repeated, cost the treasury $3,272.50 in 1931. The half million inhabitants of Washington, including Representatives and government employees, drink the excellent water supplied from city reservoirs; not so, the Senate.

Seven kinds of bottled water meet every senatorial taste. White Rock, Apollinaris, Mountain Valley, Capon Springs, Glenn Springs, Stafford Springs and Kalak appear on the bills. In addition, Pluto water is bought by the case, too. Over a six months' session, the Senate's drinking water costs about $18 a day. At the wholesale prices charged, it amounts to about five cents a glass.

To aid Senators to quaff their favorite brands of water handily, the taxpayers supply neat little bottle openers such as are found in hotel rooms for removing tops from ginger ale—and other—bottles. Like the Senators, the bottle openers must be maintained. Here is an entry, under date of December 31, 1930, among the annual spendings:

137

Acme Plating & Manufacturing Co.: 1930
Dec. 19. For nickel plating 5 bottle openers for cloak
rooms, at 50 cents, $2.50.

Hundreds of tons of ice cool the water during a session.
Bills are rendered monthly by the Chr. Heurich Brewing
Company. Winter or summer, the Senate is a good cus-
tomer. Its bill for December, 1930, for instance, was
$197.78; for May, 1931, $174.72.

Other purchases include snuff in small quantities, sand
for the sandboxes in the Senate chamber, sponges, lanterns
with red globes, and sawdust. A Washington bank is
paid $200 a year for "clearing checks." Accuracy of the
timepiece is insured by the payments of such quarterly
bills as the following:

Western Union Telegraph Company:
For standard time service for the quarter ending
December 31, as follows:
7 clocks, Senate wing of Capitol, at $5.25 . . . . . $36.75
2 clocks, Senate Chamber, at $3.75 . . . . 7.50
1 clock, Rotunda of Capitol, $7.50, less one-
half to be paid by the House of Representatives 3.75

Total $48.00

Under this arrangement it costs the Senate $16 a month
to tell the time of day, although standard time is checked
daily by another government establishment, the Naval
Observatory, which gives it free to the world. There is

another charge incidental to the Senate's time-telling: the employment of a clock-winder. He is down on the rolls at $60 a month. He is paid that sum for keeping the clocks wound. As a sideline, he repairs ailing timepieces; for that work he receives a small sum additional for each job. Sixteen dollars for the time service from the Western Union plus $60 for winding the clocks brings the total monthly expense to $76, or about $2.50 a day. Nearly $1,000 a year of the taxpayers' money thus is spent by Senators for time-keeping.

The Western Union sends other bills monthly to the Senate. Including bills of the Postal Telegraph, the Senate's telegrams cost up to $10,000 a month during a busy session. That is an average of somewhat more than $100 a month for each Senator. Telephone service, too, is extensive, and long distance calls are numerous; bills run up to $2,200 a month during the session. This does not include calls originating with the House of Representatives.

Restaurants and kitchens are maintained at public cost of more than $50,000 a year. The treasury pays the help, but does not pay for the actual food. The pay rolls during 1931 amounted to $51,998.35. At the height of the 1930-31 session the force of waiters and cooks mounted to 88 persons—almost one employee for every Senator—and the pay roll to more than $5,500. In February, 1931, kitchen and restaurant pay roll was $5,732.17.

The barber shop and baths likewise are maintained by

the treasury. Bills for shoe paste, for sharpening shears, for a shoe-shining stand and for washing and ironing hundreds of thousands of towels dot the annual spendings. Each Senator, apparently, has his own shaving mug. Here, for instance, is a bill paid by the treasury on May 29, 1931:

Union Beauty & Barber Supply (Inc.):
For following furnished the Senators' barber shop—
1931

Jan. 29	Changing name on 1 shaving mug...$	.75
Feb. 12	1 strop	2.00
	3 blackhead removers @ 15¢	.45
13	3 bottles Glovers Cure @ 60¢	1.80
24	3 barbers' coats at $2.50	7.50
25	1 bottle Nesteen	1.50
Mar. 13	3 barbers' coats at $2.50	7.50
Apr. 7	18 shaving mugs furnished from Jan. 9 to April 7, @ $1.50	27.00
Apr. 18	6 bottles Listerine @ 80¢	4.80
May 13	4 barber coats at $2.50	10.00
	Total	$63.30

Does a Senator suffer from blackheads? Into the barber shop, sir, where the latest removers will cure the case—aye, even the most savage—absolutely and positively without cost. Or maybe the Senator suffers from that distressing ailment which even his best friend hesitates to mention. This way, Senator, for your halitosis;

the cure is yours for the using. Does the Senator wish to behold himself in a faultless mirror? Come, sir, and gaze your fill; admire, too, the gilding on the frames, renewed annually at the trifling cost of about $1,000 to the treasury.

Chairmen of Senate committees are provided with clerical forces assigned to the committees. Senators who are not committee chairmen are allowed four clerks each: one at $3,900; one at $2,400; one at $2,220 and one at $1,800. A messenger at $1,800 also is provided.

Nepotism is practiced to some extent in the Senate, but apparently to less degree than in the House. Representatives are allowed $5,000 apiece for clerk hire. They may divide the sum as they wish. Recent publication of the House pay roll disclosed that some Representatives had relatives working in their offices. There is no rule or law against the practice; while there may be cases of soft snaps in such employment, it is held that members should be given all the latitude they want in selecting their employees. Speaker Garner's wife, for instance, has been his secretary for years. She does the work; figuratively, she is the Speaker's right hand. To deprive Mr. Garner of her services would handicap him greatly. A somewhat similar situation prevails in certain other offices; a general rule against the employment by a member of his wife or a relative doubtless would do as much harm as good.

Nevertheless, there are exceptions. Tales are whispered

of alleged diversion of clerk hire from Representatives' clerks to the Representatives themselves. A clerk, for instance, may be down on the pay roll for $300 a month, but under a secret arrangement with her employer hands over to him a part, say $100, of her salary—so goes the covert charge. Possibly, in a few cases, this is true. It would be almost impossible to prove it. Moreover, it is unlikely; a Representative thus would place his career at the whim of an underling. Investigation fails to bring a single instance of that kind to light.

Nepotism appears to be somewhat unusual in the Senate. The complete list of Senators' clerks on the public pay roll, with their assignment to the various Senators, as taken from the official record, shows here and there an employee whose surname is the same as that of the Senator he works for. The clerk may be the Senator's son, brother, daughter, or other relative—the record does not show. In Appendix C the list, as of June 30, 1931, is reproduced from the official pay roll, as well as a similar list covering Representatives.

The pay roll of Senate officers and employees amounted to $1,608,493.19 during the fiscal year 1931. Some Senators probably have too many employees who are paid too much money. Some undoubtedly have too few who are not paid enough. Individual cases are reported, unofficially, of an employee so valuable that the Senator contributes personally a material sum to the $3,900 maximum salary allowed by the government. One former

Senator, now dead, had a secretary who is reliably reported to have received $10,000 a year. That secretary was a wonder; he was cheap at the price. On the other hand, some Senators probably have employees who are paid much more than they are worth.

A police force, distinct from the four other police forces in Washington, is maintained for the Capitol. The cost of its maintenance is paid in part by the Senate. The Senate also maintains a carpenter shop and a garage. The latter houses a number of cars used in the mail service of the Senators, and a force of five men is maintained to keep the cars in order. For gasoline, the Senate pays from 6½ to 10 cents a gallon. A tax of two cents a gallon is levied on all fuel used in motor cars in the District of Columbia, but there is no record, in the official spendings, of the payment of this tax on more than 12,000 gallons of gasoline purchased by the Senate during the fiscal year 1931.

The Senate supplies official cars to certain employees. On June 28, 1930, the record discloses, the Secretary's office purchased a Packard automobile for $2,830, trading in a used Buick car for which an allowance of $635 was made. The bill was not paid, for reasons which do not appear on the record, until December 31, more than six months thereafter.

Again, on September 25, 1930, the Senate bought a LaSalle automobile, $2,656, for the use of the financial clerk's office. A used sedan of the same make was traded in, on an allowance of $1,150. During the same fiscal year (May 12, 1931), a third car was bought—for use of the Sergeant at Arms. It was a Packard limousine, billed at $2,300, less a credit of $288 representing the proceeds of a sale at auction of a used Hudson sedan.

Another bill, dated April 18, 1931, covers trunk and suitcase equipment for the car of the Secretary of the Senate, $80. Only fine equipment commands such a price. The record is silent as to why it was necessary.

Storage amounting to $160 a month was paid on the Senate's cars in 1931. Other items involve the use of the Senate's cars. Here, for instance, is a bill paid out of the treasury November 18:

> H. B. Leary, Jr. & Bros.:
> 1930
> Nov. 4. For payment in full for repairs to automobile of Whitney Leary damaged accidentally by collision with Buick automobile of the Secretary of the Senate, $191.29.

On the same date, the following bill also was paid:

> Emerson & Orme:
> 1930
> For following furnished the U. S. Senate for the Buick automobile of the Secretary:
> Nov. 4.   1 rear fender $14.00
>   12 rear fender bolts 1.20
>   1 hub cap 1.00

1 front axle bumper bracket........ .15
1 front axle bumper bracket........ .10
Straightening front axle 5.00
Lining up front wheels 1.25
Labor 16.10
                                   _____

Total $38.80

Details of the accident which resulted in the treasury's paying for repairs to both cars (at a time when Congress was not in session) are not disclosed in the record. The taxpayers got the bill, not the information. An overhauling and welding job on the Secretary's Buick, it likewise appears from the record, was done on September 23, six weeks, apparently, before the collision. The cost of that job was $84.55.

Surprising little charges bob up here and there without explanation so far as the record is concerned, though doubtless fully warrantable to those in authority. Thus in a bill submitted by William Price for three months' service on the financial clerk's LaSalle car, the following items appear:

Nov. 26. Express charges on silver coin from Philadelphia, $1.05.

Dec. 1. Express charges on silver coin from Denver, $2.20.

What is it all about? The bill doesn't show. Nor are details given, further than those disclosed by the bill, as to the following invoice, paid January 21, 1931, from Tom's Auto Service, Inc.:

> Jan. 20. New fenders, new rim and moulding for running board, straightening and refinishing doors and side of LaSalle car; straightening bumper; new back light and repainting body of Chevrolet car, $120.50.

That sort of bill is just a teaser. It makes one wonder. So far as the record is concerned, the wonder will never cease. The taxpayers, whose curiosity may be pardoned because they paid the bill, will never know.

Many pages of the swindle sheet have been turned. We near the end. Indeed, there is but one grouping of items left, and, appropriately, it lies near the end. That grouping covers the earthly ending of some of the members themselves, their answer to the last roll call.

Death reached into the Senate of the United States twice during the fiscal year 1931; into the House fourteen times. Sixteen members of the Congress, including the Speaker of the House, passed on. Eight employees of the Senate died during the year; eight of the House. For each member of Congress and each employee, thirty-two, all told, final funeral and other arrangements were made by the government.

The ruling passion is strong, even in death. The record bears witness to this truth in the unusual spendings for funeral and other expenses out of the public treasury.

146

House and Senate have adopted the custom of presenting to the widow or estate of each employee dying in the service a sum of money equivalent to six or twelve months' salary. It is a token of the esteem in which the services of the departed one were held. For the eight employees of the Senate who died during the year, sums totaling $16,305 thus were appropriated. They ranged from $405 to $3,360. For those employees no public funeral expenses were paid; the gratuities were designed to cover those expenses in full and to leave something remaining for the families of the dead.

Gratuities to families of House employees who died in the service totaled $7,657.25. The practice in the House differs somewhat from that in the Senate, as the House specifically designates $250 for funeral expenses of each employee, and, in addition, appropriates six months' salary, in each case, to the family or estate of the deceased. The House gratuities ranged from $682.25 to $1,500.

Appropriations for gratuities in the case of deceased employees of Congress thus totaled $23,972.25 in 1931. They were made without respect to the employee's station on the pay roll; the humblest messenger and the highest officer shared alike, under the custom. Without doubt these gratuities from the treasury softened, for a time, the blow sustained by the loss of the bread-winner of the family.

Senators and Representatives who die during their terms of service are more highly honored. Their funerals are public affairs, financed by public funds. In one case, the treasury helped to purchase a lot in a cemetery, paying two-thirds of the cost. In every case where death occurred during the period when Congress was in session a committee was appointed, usually consisting of the surviving members from the same State and sometimes other members as well, to accompany the body back to the home district.

The wholesale transportation of such committees and their attendant expenses extends the cost of such a public funeral far in excess of private costs. In the case of one Representative (not the Speaker) the public funeral expenditures exceeded $4,000. An incomplete list of expenditures for the fourteen funerals of Representatives during 1931 totals $22,514.10. The accounting for the fiscal year 1932 will show the whole cost, as some of the expenses extended over from 1931. In the case of Representatives it is the uniform practice to provide a casket costing $400.

Funeral expenses for the two Senators who died during the year totaled $5,273.10. The homes of these Senators had been fairly near Washington; otherwise the expenditure, which was composed largely of transportation and living expenses of the committee in each case, would have been much greater. In one case, the expenditure included 87 telegrams sent to various persons requesting them to act as honorary pallbearers.

Thus the hand of death, reaching into Congress, imposed a levy of $51,749.45 upon the public funds in 1931. Nor was that all. It has become the practice in Congress to vote a year's salary to the widow or estate of members dying during their terms. In the case of the two Senators, these payments, totaling $20,000, appear in the Secretary's list of expenditures during the year. They increase the Death levy to approximately $71,750.

Such gratuities do not appear in the record of House expenditures for the year. Were they to be made later (as customary) they would involve an additional expenditure of $140,000, bringing the total to about $211,750.

The practice of providing elaborate funerals for members and voting gratuities to their families, appears to be peculiar to public life. Few instances have come to light where such practice is followed in private business. The custom of paying funeral expenses of employees or of voting gratuities to their families was fairly common, however, until recently, among large business institutions.

Chapter XI

A Flash of Red

With pistols for two a House Committee swept out of Washington in the summer of 1930 looking for Reds from Moscow. Or, possibly, the pistols were bought for one man only—one of the two-gun, he-men type of the vanishing West. The records do not disclose the details; they show only that the taxpayers bought the weapons. Who toted them and when or how they were used are cloaked with official privacy.

Their purchase, however, was quite a novelty. Congressional committees, as we have seen, apparently rely mainly on other things. On plenty of money from the treasury; on batches of subpoenas; on expert stenographers; on mineral waters, houseboats, blimps, tips; on a bevy of high-salaried investigators; and, finally, on a two-ton appearance. The pistol as aid to a probe is rare.

However, a committee rampant on a field of daisies is one thing and a committee stalking bloodthirsty Reds is quite another. Caution must be observed. And caution was observed, as the following entry on the cash book, dated August 29, 1930, and written on the page of spendings, shows:

Hamilton Fish, Jr.:

Expenses for Agent James E. Amos, for railroad, etc., to Wingdale and Beacon, N. Y.	$10.00
1 S. & W. M. & P. Model No. 50417	20.00
1 Colt P. Positive .32 caliber	26.50
1 box 32/30 cartridges	1.75
1 box 32 Colt N. P. cartridges	1.18
Total	$59.43

Mr. Fish was Chairman then of the special House Committee of Five Investigating Communistic Activities in the United States. For some time previously Mr. Fish had been seeing Red, and Communistic workers were his meat. The danger that threatened the country from agitators working under the direction of the Soviet Government concerned him; it might be very real in those days of depression. Certainly it was worthy of investigation. Wasn't Moscow opposed to Capitalism? And wasn't the United States a Capitalistic country? Well, why argue?

There was a bit of argument nevertheless—two bits, in fact—in Congress before the Hamilton Fish committee was given $25,000 and the blessing of the House. It appears from the record that Mr. Fish had wanted $50,000, but that certain members of the House before whom he made his plea for the cash thought he was just fooling and cut his allowance in two. Nor were all members of the House inclined to view with alarm the Communistic threat. Some apparently thought it a false alarm. Possibly, in the meager findings of the Committee, those gentlemen chuckled when the investigation ended; but that is getting ahead of the story.

On May 22, 1930, the House voted, after some discussion, to authorize the investigation. The vote was 210 to 18, an overwhelming majority. And on June 12, Representative Perkins introduced a resolution to give the Fish Committee $25,000 for expenses.

The Perkins resolution was referred to the House Committee on Accounts and on the following day was reported to the House. Representative Warren, in the ensuing debate, asserted that according to all the evidence presented to the Committee on Accounts, the $25,000 asked for "by the so-called Fish committee is absolutely unwarranted and unnecessary." He continued:

"I thought $15,000 would be amply sufficient until the first of January. Now let's stop a minute and see about the high cost of investigations in the House. We set aside from the contingent fund every year $40,000 for investigations and special committees; yet the House has already authorized at this session investigations and authorizations to the extent of $213,736.45, leaving a deficit in the contingent fund of $173,736.45."

Representative LaGuardia of New York, speaking on the resolution, advised the House to "give some sort of study to the question of unemployment, and do it in the good American way, and in that way we will stop all need of a congressional investigation of Communistic activities."

There were others who apparently did not regard highly either the investigation or the cost. Representative Cochran of Missouri, a member of the Committee on Accounts, had this to say:

"The gentleman from New York (Mr. Fish) made a statement before the Committee on Accounts. I was immediately convinced by the statement that he was following the old policy of asking for twice the amount he wanted and if given half would be perfectly satisfied. That is what the Committee did—gave him half—but it went further.

"The resolution provides that the various agencies of the Government shall furnish this committee with members to assist in their investigation, and in my opinion if the House agrees to that provision it will be giving the Committee at least $25,000 worth of service besides $25,000 (in cash). When you transfer men from the Department of Justice, from the Secret Service, from the Department of Labor, and post office investigators to this Committee to help them along with the investigation, you are giving them the equivalent of a good many thousand dollars."

So the resolution was adopted and the Fish committee started out, in mid-June of 1930, with $25,000 at its disposal, plus the trained detective forces of the government. The personnel of the Committee, in addition to Chairman Fish, included Representatives Carl G. Bachmann, John R. Nelson, Robert S. Hall and E. E. Eslick. The five committeemen remained at Washington for three weeks after the adoption of the resolution until Congress adjourned on July 3, and soon thereafter started out to follow the Red trail wherever it might lead them.

The trail led them at once to New York; the first bill they turned into the treasury amounted to $2,684.24. The bill shows, among the entries, that during the Committee's stay in New York, its headquarters was the Hotel Commodore, at a cost of nearly $1,000. As detailed by the Sergeant at Arms of the House, the account follows:

J. G. Rodgers, Sergeant at Arms ....$	309.14
Hotel Commodore, New York City	988.94
Railroad tickets, New York to Chicago	488.30
New York to Communistic Camp, expenses..	144.80
W. L. Reynolds, clerk to committee	60.00
Representative Hall	77.35
Representative Eslick	55.00
Committee Agent	77.45
Committee Agent	127.00
D. J. Amos, Dept. of Justice	76.27
Representative Bachmann	34.25
Mr. Bachmann's railroad transportation.....	20.04
Representative Nelson	36.00
Hotel Fort Shelby, Detroit, Mich.	189.70
Total ....$	2,684.24

The Fish committee was on the job. Immediately following the above expense account was another:

Expenses of W. L. Reynolds, clerk to committee	$ 39.30
Transportation, meals, J. Spolonsky, Detroit to Chicago	33.92
Hotel Stevens in Chicago	177.97
Transportation, pullman, for members returning home	395.94
Expenses in Chicago and return to Washington	20.00
Total	$672.13

During July there were other bills as well. One for $200 covered the salary of Clerk Reynolds. Another, $98.25, was incurred at New York in various ways, including the service of subpoenas on witnesses. A third bill covered additional expenses on the trip to Chicago, $102.30, and a fourth, $299.60, was for the expert stenographers taking the testimony. All told, the Fish committee spent $4,056.52 before Congress had been in adjournment a month.

It was important business, so why bother about the cost? The Committee decided to examine closely the affairs of the Soviet commercial representatives in New York, the Amtorg Trading Corporation. As no superficial inquiry would reach the heart of the subject, the Western

Union Telegraph Company was directed to search its cablegrams and produce those sent by Amtorg during the preceding twelve months. For that service, the United States treasury paid the Western Union $193.86 on September 4, 1930. Also it occurred to the investigators that the Amtorg concern might use the wireless, so on December 12 the treasury paid the following bill:

> R.C.A. Communications (Inc.):
> Searching for and photostating radiograms required by special committee, from Moscow to Amtorg officials, $112.50.

In addition the treasury paid, on the same day, $53.26 more to the Western Union to cover the following item:

> Cost of special search for messages exchanged between Moscow (Union of Socialist Soviet Republics) and New York, or elsewhere in the United States, regarding Amtorg Trading Corporation.

But Moscow was not the only foreign capital involved. The Committee found sufficient reason to send an agent South. This gentleman, U. Grant Smith, crossed the Rio Grande and proceeded to Mexico City. He stayed in that delightful community for a time, kept his eyes open, attended to his secret mission, and returned. The taxpayers paid his bill on December 23. It was $1,106.68.

In the meantime, there were the wide open spaces of the Great West and the metropolitan centers of the Pacific Coast. Maybe the menacing Reds had spawned their deviltry there. Apparently the Committee considered the Far West an excellent hunting ground, for we find, under date of November 8, the following entry on the cashier's books:

> The Pennsylvania Railroad Co.:
> Railroad and pullman transportation, New York to San Francisco, and return, furnished for use of the Fish investigating Committee, $2,756.27.

That was just the beginning of the cost of looking for Reds in the Far West. On October 16, Sergeant at Arms Rodgers cashed the following expense account at the treasury:

Olympic Hotel, Seattle, Wash. .... $	101.40
Hotel Benson, Portland, Oregon	66.00
St. Francis Hotel, San Francisco	242.67
Hotel Alexandria, Los Angeles	195.80
Hon. Carl G. Bachmann	26.50
Hon. Hamilton Fish, Jr.	21.15
W. R. Graham, committee reporter	11.40
W. L. Reynolds, committee clerk	19.00
P. H. Crook, assistant to Sergeant at Arms..	75.00
Hon. John E. Nelson	28.00
J. G. Rodgers, Sergeant at Arms, meals on trains, extra railroad and pullman fares, automobiles, serving subpoenas, telephone and telegraph, tips, etc.	973.35
Total	$1,761.27

And on the same day, another bill:

Hotel Commodore, New York City	$ 215.09
W. L. Reynolds, Clerk of committee	245.96
Hon. E. E. Eslick	69.38
Hon. R. S. Hall	77.67
George Hill, G. W. Wood, M. Batina, special service	300.00
Hon. Carl G. Bachmann	64.00
Hotel Stevens, Chicago, Ill.	64.94
P. H. Crook	53.00
W. R. Graham, committee reporter	57.97
J. G. Rodgers	153.10
Total	$1,331.11

From those bills it would appear that the Fish committee's Western swing cost the taxpayers somewhat more than $4,500; also that the Committee had worked New York again at a cost of $1,331 additional.

And now, apparently, the Committee was going strong. It had got into its stride. The Red Menace, if any, had been located; the Committee was hot on its trail. The country was about to be saved again. The danger had been spotted, charted, and targeted; doubtless it soon would be hog-tied, tortured and exterminated. The country was becoming Red-conscious. The nation awaited the dire revelations.

In this palpitating moment of national expectation, the Committee stopped work. Why? There seemed no logical explanation, except, perhaps, that the beast of the jungle was not a beast at all. The Committee still had a good-sized slice of its $25,000 left with which to administer the *coup de grace* to the Red Menace at bay, yet neither the Red Menace nor the *coup de grace* materialized. The public, waiting for the roar of a sixteen-inch gun, presently heard a report like that of a firecracker giving up the ghost. And that was that.

All told, this grandiose hunt for a Menace that didn't exist cost the taxpayers of the United States $18,210.95 plus the pay of the federal agents detached from their routine tasks to help track the Menace down. But what was $18,210.95 in the year 1931? A bagatelle—a mere dole sufficient to feed only a few thousand unemployed for a few weeks. So lightly we may charge it off to profit or loss, according to the viewpoint, and forget it.

But there were other committees of the House active during the fiscal year 1930. For instance, the Committee on Interstate and Foreign Commerce, headed by Representative Parker of New York, concerned over the railroad situation.

Mr. Parker's Committee decided to investigate railroad holding companies. The House authorized the inquiry in the latter part of January, 1930, appropriating $25,000 therefor. The Committee employed an expert investigator, Walter W. M. Splawn, at $1,000 a month; an economist, James C. Bonbright, at $750 a month; an attorney, M. S. Breckenridge, at $312.50 a month; an assistant investigator, Willard W. Gatchell, at $250 a month; another assistant, W. H. Watts, at $220 a month; a junior economist, Norris G. Kenny, at $220 a month; and clerical workers sufficient to bring its pay roll for June up to $2,-954.17.

Then began the inquiry. The Committee's workers assigned to the various railroads went into railroad offices and looked into everything except the gold fillings in the President's mouth. From June, 1930, to March 3, 1931, inclusive, the Committee spent $28,348.81 in salaries. In addition, it spent $4,696.24 for expenses of Messrs. Splawn and his staff, the sum including expenses of members of the Committee. All told, it distributed $33,045.05 of the taxpayers' money. In return, it yielded a prodigious report—three volumes of statistics, documents, names, and what have you. It probably is a perfectly safe gamble that not one member of Congress in ten has read it.

Some of the Committee's spendings for expenses leave the casual taxpayer bewildered. Here, for example, a minor item, is a bill of the Chesapeake & Potomac Telephone Company for certain long distance calls from Washington:

Morgan calling Splawn in New York ....$ 1.40
Splawn calling Cat. 4820 in New York 1.05
Splawn calling Splawn in New York 1.05
Splawn calling Rayburn in Bonham 10.50
Splawn calling Cat. 4820 in New York .... .90
Splawn calling Rayburn in Bonham 10.50

Splawn calling Splawn in New York 2.10
Splawn calling Interstate in New York 3.15
Splawn calling Splawn in New York 5.60
Gatchell calling Stone in New York 1.40

$37.65
Credit Sept. 22 .... 1.40

Total $36.25

That bill was paid October 7. Three times, it appears, did Splawn in Washington call Splawn in New York. Splawn calling unto Splawn cost the taxpayers $8.75 during the period covered. Is it possible that Mr. Splawn was talking to himself over the long distance wires? There appears no other Splawn, save the $1,000-a-month investigator, on the pay roll. Yet there were Splawns at each end. It is all quite foggy; but, of course, it must have been entirely proper and legal or the treasury wouldn't have paid it.

Spanking a naughty Judge was another item that cost the taxpayers upwards of $8,000 during the fiscal year. The official in question was Harry B. Anderson, United States District Judge for Western Tennessee, whose conduct in office was investigated by a House committee. On June 12, 1930, when the investigation was authorized, Representative Hickey, who called up the resolution, stipulated that the cost should not exceed $5,000.

The Committee hired two expert investigators, E. E.

Conroy and F. J. Kilmartin, at $15 and $11 a day, respectively, and sent them to Memphis. Later a third investigator, H. J. Flesher, at $8 a day, was added to the pay roll. Thus at $34 a day plus expenses the investigation proceeded. Representatives LaGuardia, Sumners and Hickey appear in the cash account occasionally for their expenses. None of the individual expense accounts exceeded $500 (the highest was $452.73 covering Mr. Kilmartin's salary and expenses from November 11 to December 1) but there were forty-four separate bills to pay during the five months' inquiry. The total cost was $8,-473.78—a fairly stiff charge for the formal censure which Judge Anderson ultimately received. So in the end Representative Hickey's $5,000 stipulation turned to be less than sixty percent of the actual spendings.

The House actually paid out in 1931 for its investigations $112,381, or less than one-fourth of the amount spent by the Senate for such investigations. Both Houses expended, under that heading, somewhat more than $600,000 during the year. Probably one-half of that amount was dribbled out in extravagances and useless inquiries. If so, the waste was equivalent to the annual interest, at the rate paid by the government, on a loan of $10,000,000.

Other intriguing items bob up occasionally in the long listing of the House spendings, minor chords contributing to the medley of waste on Capitol Hill at Washington.

Echoes of other days rebound from time to time from the treasury in 1931. Here is such an instance:

> Riggs National Bank:
> Rental of 2 safe-deposit vaults, Apr. 17, 1925, to September 26, 1930, for storing certain papers belonging to the Treasury Department, used in connection with investigation of alleged duplicate bonds in the Sixty-eighth Congress by the Committee on Banking and Currency, $816.68.

Remember the bond scandal? Or, rather, what threatened to become the bond scandal? It stalked into the early days of the Harding Administration with whispers and rumors that a mammoth steal had been made from the United States treasury through duplicate Liberty Bonds. Harding studied the evidence and at once suspended the head of the Bureau of Engraving and Printing and a number of his aides. Director Wilmeth and his subordinates, President Harding let it be known, were accused of nothing improper; there were other reasons for the suspension which the White House deemed good and sufficient.

An investigation was started and for a time both White House and country were quite nervous. Later the case was smoothed over and hushed up. One by one the suspended officials and employees were reinstated—all save Director Wilmeth who then had found congenial employment and preferred the hazards of private business to the kindness of public officials. The case was closed without the public's being told exactly what had happened, and in time it was almost forgotten.

Now, in this buried item in House Document No. 2, made public in January, 1932, were taps sounded over the corpse. It is significant of the state of the congressional mind that a private safe-deposit vault was rented in Washington's leading bank to store the papers. Directly across Pennsylvania Avenue from the Riggs National Bank lies the United States Treasury, and in the Treasury are the finest and most modern vaults in the world. Yet the investigating committee, for some reason of its own, went to the bank over the way. Then the committee allowed them to remain in the private bank for more than five years. As usual, the public treasury got it in the neck. Fortunately the charge was small.

Some of the spendings listed in the House account are cryptic. On April 3 there appears this item: "postage for memorial service in the House of Representatives, $18." Postage for a memorial service—how? One wonders. Another entry, repeated several times on varying dates, covers the purchase of "12 gallons of Pep, $24," for the use of the House. Pep? For what use? Certainly not for use in speeding legislation. The bill came from a chemical company; possibly the Pep described was for cleaning purposes rather than for lethargic solons.

Representatives, like Senators, fairly often believe they have been cheated out of their dues at election time.

Especially when the count is close are such claims made. Five seats were contested in the fiscal year 1931. The House paid the bills in each case; the total cost to the taxpayers of the five contests was $15,778.23. Three of the contests cost the limit of $4,000 each—$2,000 to each contestant. The other two were less expensive. Mrs. Ruth Bryan Owen, the successful contestant in one of these cases, turned in a bill for only $36.40 to cover her expenses, as compared with a bill of $1,458.33 paid by the treasury for her opponent, William C. Lawson. Mrs. Owen could have run up a bill for the limit of $2,000 allowed, but she preferred, from a sense of fitness, to hold the costs down.

The sixth case, originating in Indiana, was a contest between Louis Ludlow and Ralph E. Updike. In that case, as in the Owen-Lawson case, the limit was not reached. Mr. Ludlow's expenses of $1,033.50 were but little more than half of the customary allotment. Those of his opponent were slightly higher, amounting to $1,250.

There is some justification, perhaps, for the payment by the treasury of modest sums to defray costs of a contest. Many members of Congress have little more than their salaries and the cost of a contest is beyond their personal means. At the same time, the general public, which places the taxes in the treasury, has only a mild interest, at best, in these isolated fights. No better method of financing them than from the public treasury yet has been devised, however.

We have glimpsed the cost of folding and mailing speeches delivered in Congress, the work being done by a force of young men and women who are paid, as a rule, $1 a thousand copies for all they fold. The extent to which these gems of oratory are broadcast over the United States is indicated by entries in the House spendings showing that the treasury paid $423.52 for string and twine alone to bind the bulky bales of speeches. Four hundred and twenty-three dollars will buy many a mile of string and twine at wholesale prices; yet every yard was needed during the year. Here, it would seem, is a palpable waste of public funds, not alone of the relatively small change paid for twine, but of the much larger sums it costs to frank these effusions through the mails. It ought to be stopped. Almost any member of Congress will agree to that, yet little has been done to lessen this waste of the taxpayers' money.

Another expensive practice is that of summoning witnesses from afar to Washington to testify before investigating committees. That is less common, as nearly all committees now go to the hinterland to conduct their investigations. Yet it persists to some degree, as witness the payment of $541.95 to three witnesses testifying in July, 1930, before the House Committee on Banking and Currency.

One of the witnesses came from Oklahoma City. His railroad and pullman fare amounted to $200.55. The second came from Bowling Green, Ky., and had a transportation bill of $90.98. The third witness came on from Fergus Falls, Minn., at a transportation cost of $196.42. They remained in Washington three days, each being paid $18 for subsistence. Thus these three witnesses, Messrs. C. G. Shull, Max B. Nahm and Elmer E. Adams, not only cost the government more than $500, but lost at least five days apiece from their own affairs. For that lost time they received no compensation.

In minor items of maintenance, the House bills contain fewer unusual charges than those of the Senate. On the other hand, some of the things for which the House spends the taxpayers' money appear with robust price tags. Carpet for Representatives' offices is one of these. It cost $4.42 per square yard, with borders costing $2.21 per square yard. Only a few rooms each year require new floor coverings, yet the charge for these few rooms is considerable. One bill, covering work in twelve rooms, amounted to $2,317.92; another to $3,264.12. The whole cost probably averages $10,000 a year. Why such expensive floor coverings?

But it is in the House stationery shop that one glimpses unusual items. The stationery shop is designed to supply Representatives with such articles as they require in their official correspondence; and, as shown, each Representative starts the year with a credit of $125 at the shop. Yet the bills for supplies sold the Representatives on those credits covers such odds and ends as pedometers, alarm clocks (by the dozen), book ends, nail clippers, antique time pieces, knives and manicure scissors. In 1931 the bills also included fourteen cedar chests, six dressers, five dressing tables and eight beds, complete.

From this stock the thrifty Representative, economizing on his stationery, could select, if he desired, a cedar chest, a bed, a dressing table or a dresser. Oh, yes; for use, of course, in conducting his official correspondence. That's what the $125 stationery allowance is for—that and nothing else.

At least, such is the theory.

Chapter XII

Pinching Pennies at the White House

Back in the good old days when it mattered not whether steak cost forty cents a pound or sixty, the White House roof decided to fall. The aging timbers first indicated their purpose to certain architects and engineers in the government service. Whereupon there was a great to-do; roof doctors held clinics and consultations; the treasury was warned to loosen its grasp on a few hundred thousands; and a new roof was prescribed.

So it came about that on a certain Friday morning early in the Fall of 1924, Budget Director Lord hurried across the narrow street separating the White House from the treasury on his way to the President. Between the President and his great chief of finance there was deep and sincere sympathy. The blue of his native Maine skies was mirrored in General Lord's kindly eyes; the conservatism of New England with its cautious carefulness in all things surged through his veins with every heartbeat, just as it surged through the veins of his chief; frugality bred by the grudging fields and inhospitable climate of his youth was the very twin of Coolidge economy, rooted in Vermont.

Yet, withal, these innate promptings were not upper-most today. His friend, the President, was in danger. Hastily an estimate had been prepared of the cost of a new roof; and eagerly the item had been included in the estimate of White House spendings which General Lord carried at that moment under his left arm.

The papers were placed before the President. The items covered the whole range of White House spend-ings proposed for the next fiscal year. Mr. Coolidge scanned them all with an occasional word of comment until the unusual entry, "Extraordinary Repairs, White House Roof," was reached. There he stopped and, swing-ing around in his swivel chair, asked for an explanation. It was given.

"No," said Mr. Coolidge.

"But, Mr. President," pleaded the Budget Director, "you are in danger. The roof may fall at any time!"

General Lord was an eloquent man, as those who have heard his radio addresses, can testify. And now he made a generous draft upon his talent. For more than a century the stout timbers, hewn from the Virginia woods, had served the nation. They had sheltered the great Mon-roe. They had held back the storms of heaven from those other storms that beat down on the fair head of Peggy O'Neill. They had caught the mirth and the deep pathos of the immortal Lincoln. They had echoed the laughter of Frances Folsom on her wedding day and they had mantled the tragedy of Woodrow Wilson.

"Now, Mr. President," the Budget Director concluded, "they are rotting away. They have served. They must be replaced, or the time is near when the world will sorrow in another White House tragedy."

The President appeared visibly affected. For a full minute he said nothing. Then his lips parted.

"How much time?" he asked.

"A few months, perhaps. Maybe a year. More likely, two years. Conceivably, five years. Even the experts cannot tell."

"How much money?" the President inquired.

"Four hundred thousand dollars."

Mr. Coolidge picked up his pencil and reached for a pad of paper. Pencil met pad. Squinting down through his glasses, General Lord's eyes saw the Coolidge pencil fashion a dollar mark. Then a figure, 4. Then five ciphers, thus—$400,000. Under the $400,000, Mr. Coolidge wrote the figure 6. Under that he drew a line. Then he multiplied $400,000 by 6, fixed the decimal point in its proper place and faced his Budget Director.

"Twenty-four thousand dollars is the interest at 6 percent on $400,000 for one year. For two years it comes to $48,000."

He reached for General Lord's carefully typed estimates and drew a heavy black line through the $400,000 item.

"I'm asking everybody in the government to cut spendings," he said quietly. "I can't add $400,000 to my own. Come back with it in two years."

For some time thereafter the President lived under a rotting roof. Many a formal dinner, many a gathering attended by the nation's élite who knew nothing of the danger, was held before General Lord came back at the end of the two years. Then the President somewhat reluctantly agreed to include the item—in the following year's estimates. By practicing what he preached—the simple doctrine of economy in public spendings—Calvin Coolidge saved the public treasury the interest on $400,000 for at least three years.

What has his successor done? Herbert Hoover has compelled his subordinates in the federal government to cut the spendings of their various departments, boards and commissions, by hundreds of millions of dollars. Has he cut his own?

The record shows he has not. To the contrary, the amount spent to maintain the White House establishment during the fiscal year 1931 reached the highest level, for routine expenditures, ever recorded in the history of the United States.

What the White House spent in that regard for 1932 has not been made public in detail as this is written. Appropriations for the fiscal year 1932 (which closed June 30, 1932) were greater, however, than actual spendings for the fiscal year 1931.

In December, 1931, Mr. Hoover transmitted the Budget estimates for 1933 to Congress. Those estimates included the proposed spendings of every branch of the government. They had been cut below original requests by approximately $300,000,000 so far as the executive establishment was concerned. Yet Mr. Hoover, with the exception of one item which was reduced by $5,000 from the estimated spendings of 1932, asked Congress to appropriate for the White House in 1933 the identical amounts appropriated for 1932.

Apparently, Mr. Hoover's urge for decreased spendings did not extend—except for the single item mentioned— to his own personal establishment. Lower spendings everywhere, except in the White House itself—such was the record.

Mr. Hoover didn't get what he asked for. Where the President had spared the pruning knife, the House and Senate used it. The White House appropriations were cut. They were brought into line with the ideas of economy which had been applied to every branch of the federal government. Congress did the cutting, however, and not the President. Here is where the cutting was done:

Personal services in the office of the President, cut from $96,180 requested by Mr. Hoover to $90,000.

Traveling and official entertainment expenses of the President, cut from the $25,000 requested to $20,000.

Other traveling expenses and repairs and maintenance of the White House and grounds, cut from the $142,000 sought by the President to $125,000.

Printing and binding of White House documents, etc., cut from $2,700 requested by Mr. Hoover to $2,000.

Contingent expenses, covering stationery, books, telephones, automobile and garage expenses, and so on, cut from $43,500 to $35,000.

The Budget, submitted by Mr. Hoover to Congress in December, 1931, contains the following record of White House spendings:

> Expenses of the Office of the President, actual spendings in 1931, $121,029; estimated spendings in 1932, $126,180; amount requested for 1933, $126,180.
>
> Contingent Expenses of the Executive Office, actual spendings in 1931, $43,491; estimated spendings in 1932, $43,500; amount requested for 1933, $43,500.
>
> Printing and Binding, Executive Office, actual spendings in 1931, $2,700; estimated spendings in 1932, $2,700; amount requested for 1933, $2,700.
>
> Traveling Expenses (and official entertainment) of the President, actual spendings in 1931, $25,000; estimated spendings in 1932, $25,000; amount requested for 1933, $25,000.
>
> Total, Executive Office proper, including $75,000 salary of the President and $15,000 salary of the Vice President, actual spendings in 1931, $282,220; estimated spendings in 1932, $287,380; amount requested for 1933, $287,380.

One other item of White House spendings remains. It covers the maintenance of the White House and its grounds. Actual spendings in 1931 were $135,000; estimated spendings in 1932 were $147,000; and the amount requested for 1933 was $142,000. Here, for the first time, the Budget discloses a voluntary cut in the spendings of the President's immediate establishment. It amounts to $5,000 in the care and maintenance of the Executive Mansion and its grounds. At the same time, the amount requested for 1933 was $7,000 more than was actually spent in 1931.

White House spendings have risen right merrily during the stressful years since Herbert Hoover became President. In 1931 they had increased by more than $100,000, or nearly one-third, over spendings during the last full year of the Coolidge Administration. These figures refer only to routine spendings and do not consider the extraordinary expense of repairing the Executive Offices after the fire in 1930, which amounted to $188,061.

The fiscal year 1928 marked the last full twelve-month of Mr. Coolidge's term as President. During that year the White House spendings totaled $342,029, including the White House police force, its salaries and equipment. Including the police, Mr. Hoover's occupancy of the White House in 1931 resulted in spendings of $445,693, exclusive of his $75,000 salary.

In 1930, the first full year of Mr. Hoover's administration, White House spendings were $439,373. The first full year of the Hoover administration witnessed a jump in spendings of more than $60,000—nearly one-sixth—

over the year when his predecessor turned over the keys to him.

There were various reasons. Take, for instance, the single item of traveling expenses and official entertaining at the White House. For many years Congress has appropriated $25,000 annually to cover that. The money is available for spending just as the President may direct and need be accounted for only by his certificate. But the law does not require the President to spend the full $25,000; and until Mr. Hoover entered the White House no President for eighteen years with the single exception of Taft (in the campaign year of 1912) had spent the full amount. Each year a part of the $25,000 had been returned to the treasury.

Mr. Hoover changes the established practice. Instead of returning some part of the $25,000 to the treasury during his first full year of office, the fiscal year 1930, Mr. Hoover spent all, and more. The record discloses the total spent at $28,121.47. The following year, 1931, the actual spendings were exactly $25,000. Not a dime went back to the treasury, if the official Budget may be believed. For 1932, as the Budget estimates of spendings read, the full $25,000 will be spent. And for 1933, Mr. Hoover planned to spend $25,000 once more—till Congress lopped off $5,000 and gave him but $20,000.

The Hoover spendings—$25,000 for 1931, $28,121 for 1930—compare with spendings in other fiscal years as follows:

Coolidge and Hoover, one fiscal year
1929.............$24,432

Calvin Coolidge's Administration
1928.............$22,145
1927............. 18,441
1926............. 24,576
1925............. 22,815

Harding and Coolidge, one fiscal year
1924.............$21,427

Warren Harding's Administration
1923.............$ 9,888
1922............. 12,349

Wilson and Harding, one fiscal year
1921.............$ 3,092

Woodrow Wilson's Administration
1920.............$24,736
1919............. 13,305
1918............. 5,125
1917............. 19,866
1916............. 18,654
1915............. 9,235
1914............. 13,067

Taft and Wilson, one fiscal year
1913.............$21,998

Another reason why White House spendings were higher in 1931 than ever before revolves around the conduct of the Executive Offices and their force of 37 workers, including the President's three secretaries.

177

Mr. Hoover was the first President to desire more than one Secretary so urgently as to have Congress increase the number. Mr. Coolidge managed with one Secretary who drew $7,500 a year until the beginning of the fiscal year 1927. And then Mr. Coolidge did not ask Congress to increase his Secretary's salary; the salary was lifted when Congress decided to boost the pay of its own members from $7,500 to $10,000 apiece, and to give the Cabinet officials $15,000 annually instead of the $12,000 they had been receiving. Quite without Mr. Coolidge's knowledge, it is said, the same bill authorized an increase in salary from $7,500 to $10,000 for the President's Secretary.

The bill passed Congress with a whoop in the winter of 1926. The increases were not effective, however, until the first day of the following July, when the next fiscal year started. It was in that manner that Mr. Everett Sanders, Chairman of the Republican National Committee but then Secretary to President Coolidge, got his raise in pay.

Joseph P. Tumulty, Woodrow Wilson's efficient Secretary, received but $7,500. President Harding's Secretary, Mr. Christian, received $7,500. Prior to Mr. Hoover's inauguration, the government had paid $7,500 a year in salary and no more to the Secretary to the President, except during the last two and two-thirds years of the Coolidge Administration. When Mr. Hoover took office the expenditure jumped to $30,000 a year for three Secretaries at $10,000 apiece.

Workers in the Executive Offices have remained fairly constant at from 34 to 38 since the time of Roosevelt. The pay roll, of course, has risen. In the last full year of the Coolidge Administration, 1928, Executive Office salaries, exclusive of those of the President and Vice-President, totaled $93,228. In 1930, the first full year of the Hoover Administration, the salary roll was $122,888. That was a jump of nearly $30,000—almost one-fourth —in two years. In 1931, the total ebbed back to $121,029, but the Budget estimate of 1932 spendings pushes it forward again to $126,180—highest on record, and nearly two-thirds as much again as the wartime spendings of Woodrow Wilson in that particular.

Here is the record for the last 20 years, as disclosed by official treasury figures, for Executive Office salaries:

1931	$121,029
1930	122,888
1929	101,620
1928	93,228
1927	93,469
1926	91,956
1925	92,800
1924	81,849
1923	79,700
1922	72,610
1921	77,758
1920	78,746
1919	76,094
1918	76,311

1917	76,020
1916	73,188
1915	70,490
1914	69,206
1913	67,891
1912	65,933

Three Secretaries instead of one, each with a White House automobile and chauffeur, likewise have contributed in some measure to the increase in the contingent expenses of the White House. The automobiles are not bought by the government, but are lent by various manufacturers without charge to the President. That is done not only from good will, but for the prestige accruing to the various makes of cars, although the manufacturers are forbidden to advertise the fact that their product is used at the White House. The upkeep of the cars, however, is paid for out of the treasury and appears in the White House Contingent Expenses, thus officially defined in The Budget:

> Contingent Expenses: For contingent expenses of the Executive Office, including stationery, record books, telegrams, telephones, books for library, furniture and carpets for offices, automobiles, expenses of garage, including labor, special services, and miscellaneous items, to be expended in the discretion of the President.

Until Mr. Hoover became President, the White House Contingent Expenses had never exceeded $35,000, with the exception of the fiscal years 1923 and 1924 when they were $37,288 and $37,632, respectively. In Woodrow Wilson's mid-term, 1916, the item dropped to $20,612. President Coolidge held the annual spendings at $34,730 from 1925 to 1928, inclusive. In the fiscal year 1929, during which Mr. Hoover was President for nearly four months, White House Contingent Expenses totaled $34,995. Thereafter:

1930	$41,000
1931	43,491
1932 (estimated)	43,500

The estimate for 1932 is contained in The Budget, and an appropriation was made by Congress for the full amount. For 1933 President Hoover requested an appropriation of $43,500 again, but Congress cut the amount to $35,000.

More White House policemen to protect Mr. Hoover likewise swell the spendings. In 1923, Warren Harding had a force of 33 men which cost the government $62,735. By 1925 the force had grown to 39 and the cost to $78,840. The number remained at 39 during the Coolidge Administration, although the total cost advanced to an average of about $85,700 a year. In 1930, first full year of the Hoover régime, the number still was 39 and the cost was $85,900. In 1931, it was increased to 48 men and the cost advanced to $118,473. The foregoing figures do not include Secret Service men detailed to guard the person of the President, although at the present time the uniformed police force is under the Secret Service.

The White House police are not entered on the budget for the Executive Mansion, but appear under Treasury Department spendings.

One of the larger items of White House spendings covers the maintenance of the White House itself and the upkeep of the grounds. Since the last full year of Wilson's Administration, when sheep were used instead of lawn mowers to keep the White House grass clipped, this item has virtually doubled in cost. The treasury records show that in 1920 the total spendings were $68,616; in 1931, $135,000. For 1933, Mr. Hoover requested $142,000, but Congress reduced the spendings to $125,000.

That means, perhaps, fewer flowers for White House tables, fewer employees and a cut here and there in miscellaneous spendings. As defined in The Budget, the item covers spendings:

> For the care, maintenance, repair and alteration, refurnishing, improvement, heating, and lighting, including electric power and fixtures of the Executive Mansion, the Executive Mansion greenhouses, including reconstruction, and the Executive Mansion grounds, and traveling expenses, to be expended as the President may determine notwithstanding the provisions of any other Act.

In 1931, 60 employees received their wages and salaries under this item of White House spendings. Warren Harding had maintained 62 workers. Coolidge cut the number to 55 during the one year of his Administration. During the Coolidge Administration the spendings under this heading averaged $107,000 a year. In 1929, when Mr. Hoover moved into the White House and Mr. Coolidge moved out, the spendings jumped from $103,443 (in 1928) to $129,186. In 1930, they jumped again, to $158,764 (highest on record), exclusive of extraordinary repairs occasioned by the fire of that year. In 1931, the spendings receded to $135,000, and in 1932, the Budget estimates, the total will be $147,000.

The White House force is headed by a manager at $3,000 a year. Next to him comes the assistant director of gardens at $2,800. Four foremen mechanics are down at $2,400 each. The chief cook gets $1,920; three other cooks draw from $1,080 to $1,320; there are two butlers, at $1,440 and $1,200; a valet at $1,800; five pantrymen at from $1,080 to $1,230; a steward's helper at $1,260; a kitchen maid, a chambermaid, and a laundress at from $1,020 to $1,080, and five maids at $936.

Likewise, there are a gardener at $1,680 and five assistants at $1,524; a painter at $1,740 and a plumber at $1,680; a mechanic at $1,500; two footmen at $1,320; a handyman at $1,080 and 12 laborers at from $1,140 to $1,500. Their combined salaries amounted to $84,400 in 1931, in addition to which temporary employees were hired at a cost of $14,798. Wages and salaries in keeping up the White House and grounds thus aggregated $99,-198 during the year.

A total of $35,802 was spent, in addition, in 1931 for other White House expenses chief of which were the following:

Supplies and materials $16,248
Electricity 443
Repairs and alterations 5,151
Special and miscellaneous current expenses.... 3,606
Equipment 5,982
Structures and nonstructural improvements... 4,202

All told, routine White House spendings in 1931, not including the President's salary, totaled $445,693. That figure includes the White House police force, but does not include the plain-clothes Secret Service men. Comparable figures extend back through the Budget for nine years. They are as follows:

1931....................$445,693
1930.................... 439,373
1929.................... 378,862
1928.................... 342,029
1927.................... 343,342
1926.................... 347,394
1925.................... 340,572
1924.................... 318,293
1923.................... 289,330

184

Beyond 1923, the figures are not comparable as they do not include the White House police which then were under the local government of the District of Columbia. Excluding that item however, White House spendings in 1922 were $206,658 and in 1921 were $193,213.

A rise in the cost of maintaining the White House from $289,330 under Warren Harding in 1923 to $445,693 under Herbert Hoover represents an additional cost of $156,363 a year to the taxpayers. Measured against the great outlays for other branches of the government, the sum is picayunish. Only the proportion looms large; the increase amounts to 54 percent. Whatever branches of government cut their costs, the White House was not among them.

Let us follow the proportion through and see where it would have led had the other branches of the federal establishments done likewise in augmenting their spendings.

In 1923, when the White House cost $289,330 to maintain, the ordinary running expenses of the entire federal establishment, according to the Budget, amounted to $3,532,269,266.

By 1931, the White House spendings had increased 54 percent. Had the entire federal establishment increased its spendings by 54 percent, the cost of running the government in 1931 would have amounted to $5,439,694,670. However, the actual spendings totaled only $3,987,611,353. The entire government spendings during those eight years increased somewhat less than 13 percent, the proportion of increase being less than one-fourth of the proportion of increase in the spendings of the White House alone.

In other words, had the rest of the government followed the White House lead in spending, which fortunately for the nation it did not do, the American treasury would have been called on to pay out $1,452,083,317 more than it did pay out, and the deficit at the close of the year would have approximated $2,350,000,000 instead of $900,000,000.

There would seem to be no apparent reason why the policy of retrenchment enforced upon the great spending branches of the government should not apply equally to the White House itself. The official figures, however, disclose that it did not apply. The White House preached economy—for others.

Chapter XIII

Government by Commission

"There being no disagreement as to the need of farm relief," wrote Herbert Hoover in the spring of 1929, "the problem before us becomes one of method by which relief may be most successfully brought about. * * * There is no single plan or principle that can be generally adopted. * * * I have long held that the multiplicity of causes of agricultural depression could only be met by the creation of a great instrumentality clothed with sufficient power and resources to assist our farmers to meet these problems, each upon its own merits.

"The creation of such an agency would at once transfer the agricultural question from the field of politics into the realm of economics and would result in constructive action. The Administration is pledged to create an instrumentality that will investigate the causes, find sound remedies and have the authority and resources to apply those remedies."

So, in advocating the first of the many Hoover Commissions, Boards and Committees, did the President advise Congress in his Message read before House and Senate on April 16, 1929. The date is important, for Mr.

187

Hoover had been inaugurated less than six weeks previously. In keeping with the platform pledge adopted at Kansas City, he was about to apply the real and genuine remedy to the financial ailments of the long-suffering farmers of America. He was in haste to apply it; in such haste that he had summoned Congress in special session.

And now Congress was to fashion the "great instrumentality" Mr. Hoover advocated. Five months in the future lay the first disastrous crash in the stock market which was to usher in the country's greatest depression; but of that catastrophe and its imminence no one in authority at Washington, apparently, was remotely apprehensive.

"The pledged purpose of such a Federal Farm Board," Mr. Hoover's message to Congress continued, "is reorganization of the marketing system on sounder and more stable and more economic lines. * * * Certain safeguards must naturally surround these (the Board's) activities, and the instrumentalities that are created. Certain vital principles must be adhered to in order not to undermine initiative. There should be no fee or tax imposed upon the farmer. No government agency should engage in the buying and selling and price fixing of products, for such course can lead only to bureaucracy and domination. * * *

"The difficulties of agriculture cannot be cured in a day; they cannot all be cured by legislation; they cannot be cured by the federal government alone. But farmers and their organizations can be assisted to overcome these inequalities. Every effort of this character is an experiment and we shall find through our experience the way to further advance. We must make a start. With the creation of a great instrumentality of this character of a strength and importance equal to that of those which we have created for transportation and banking we give immediate assurance of the determined purpose of the government to meet the difficulties of which we are now aware and to create an agency through which constructive action for the future will be assured."

There was more to the message, but such, in its essentials, was the outline of the first and greatest of the Hoover Boards. An eager Congress listened attentively, cheered, and made the Farm Board Bill the first order of business in both House and Senate. Indeed, the Bill was No. 1 in both Houses. From Democratic Texas (but lately voting for Hoover in the electoral college), New England, the Middle West, the Far West and the Old South, members of Congress united in speeding the creation of the Board the President desired.

"Eureka! We have found it after eight long years of trying!" exclaimed an enthusiastic Representative from Ohio on the floor of the House when the President's proposal was under debate. A few hesitant voices were raised to express doubt but they were smothered by the chorus of approval. "Hoover has found the remedy and I am delighted to let him lead the way!" These words, uttered on the floor of the House, bespoke the overwhelming sentiment of both House and Senate.

And so the bill was enacted into law and the Federal Farm Board came into being, with the President's glowing approval, on June 15, 1929. The members of the Board were named soon after the passage of the law; and without delay the newly created "great instrumentality" through which "constructive action for the future will be assured" got busy with $500,000,000 placed by Congress in its hands to help cure the farmer's ills.

No puny, teetering branch of the government was Mr. Hoover's first commission, but a giant from birth. It came into existence with nine members, down on the federal pay roll at $12,000 a year apiece. Vast powers were placed in the hands of those members, including the power to insure farm cooperatives against loss from declines in the prices of their products. That, too, was written into the law. And the power to organize its working forces, without limit as to salary, likewise was conferred by Congress on the Board.

Commissions were no novelty to Hoover. "During 1927, for example," says *Editorial Research Reports,* "over 1,200 group conferences of officials of the Department of Commerce and representatives of leading industrial and commercial organizations were held for the purpose of considering problems of industry, commerce, and transportation; and 343 permanent committees were created to give advice and assistance to the department in the performance of its work." That was while Hoover was head of the Department. Small wonder, then, that his faith in commissions was great.

More than 150 names went onto the Farm Board's pay roll during the fiscal year 1930, but the Board even then had not got into its true stride. The record shows that in the following year—the twelve months beginning July 1, 1930—367 persons were drawing salaries that totaled $899,000. At the top of the list stood the general counsel, at $20,000 a year. Then came the remaining eight members of the board, down at $12,000, and next to them high-powered economists and specialists, listed, in part, as follows:

Secretary, $8,500.
Head agricultural economist, field service, $6,800.
Head agricultural economist, Washington, $6,500.
Two head economists, Washington, at $6,500.
Head attorney, Washington, $6,500.
Chief of section, Washington, $6,000.
Four field representatives, at $6,000.
Six principal agricultural economists at $5,667.
Principal examiner, $5,600.
Fourteen economists at from $4,600 to $5,400.
Three field representatives at from $4,600 to $5,400.
Three experts at $4,600 to $6,500.
Five field examiners at from $4,200 to $4,500.

and more than 300 economists, attorneys, statisticians, experts, field representatives, examiners and other employees whose salaries ranged from $1,200 a year (in the case of one clerk and one stenographer) up to $5,000 apiece.

Here was the application, on a large scale, of economics to agriculture. In addition to its pay roll, the Board had certain other administrative charges, notably $100 a day for printing and binding, about $70 a day for telephones and telegrams, $90 a day for stationery and other supplies, and $221,000 during the year for travel expense. The cost of conducting the Board's affairs in 1931 was $1,727,000.

Its loans were made with lavish hand. During the first fiscal year of its existence, the Board lent $227,109,976 to farm cooperatives and received back $36,053,907 during the year. The net outgo in 1930 thus was $191,056,069. In 1931, the lending business improved: the Budget figures place the Board's total loans that year at $470,-487,579. That, it will be recalled, was a year of rapidly declining prices; the Board succeeded, however, in getting back $280,776,668 during the year, leaving net outstanding loans at $189,710,911. In 1932, according to the Budget figures, the Board expected to lend $400,000,000 and hoped to get $385,000,000 of it back. And in 1933 the plan was to lend $460,000,000 more and receive back about $325,000,000.

In actual loans this Hoover Commission distributed $697,500,000 in 1930 and 1931; its program for 1932 and 1933 called for lending $860,000,000 more, making a grand total of approximately $1,550,000,000, the greater part of which it had hopes of recovering. Some part of these gigantic loans, made in furtherance of the policy "through which constructive action for the future will be assured" undoubtedly will be lost forever, and these the taxpayers will have to make good. In the meantime, the Board expanded. Its appropriations for 1932 provided for pay rolls totaling $1,374,000 as compared with $899,000 for 1931; for a $260,000 travel fund, instead of $221,000; and for a total administrative outlay of $1,-815,000.

For 1933, even greater expansion was contemplated. It mattered not, apparently, that the Board had poured many millions down various ratholes in loans on commodities whose prices had shriveled miserably. Nor did it matter that the country was groaning beneath inordinate taxes. Nor that business was prostrate and that industrial stagnation becalmed American commerce. These regrettable developments swerved the first of the Hoover Commissions by not a hair's breadth from its predetermined course. Nor did they impel the author of the "great instrumentality" to have a heart for the struggling taxpayer. The President sent his estimates to Congress in December, 1931, asking for an increase to $1,880,000 for the Farm Board's administrative expenses in 1933.

Congress sank the pruning knife so deep into that estimate that the bewildered Board shut up offices almost completely for the first ten days of the fiscal year 1933 (July 1 to 10, 1932) and rent the air with moans and lamentations. What was it coming to—oh, what in the name of Heaven, was it coming to? To almost everyone except its own personnel and a dwindling squad of faithful friends, it seemed perfectly apparent that the Farm Board was coming to an overdue and unmourned end.

Looking back on the record of this prize commission, it is difficult even for its best friends to envision any accomplishment of real benefit to the farmer. Its best friends, by the way, include the professional ring of parlor farmers staffed and headquartered at Washington who are more skilled at using the mimeograph than the hoe. These political farmers now foresee the axe and the chopping block.

What has happened to agriculture while this "great instrumentality" designed to assure "constructive action for the future" has scattered a billion and a half dollars broadcast? Where is the "constructive action"? The Department of Agriculture's official record as of the day the Farm Board law was approved, June 15, 1929, and three years later, June 15, 1932, shows what has happened to prices. The official comparison follows:

Oats were selling for 39.3 cents per bushel in 1929; for 19.8 cents in 1932. The decline was nearly 50 percent.

Corn was selling for 86.9 cents per bushel in 1929; in 1932, for 29.4 cents; the decline was more than 65 percent.

Wheat was selling for 86.8 cents per bushel in

1929; in 1932, for 37.3 cents; the decline was nearly 60 percent.

Cotton was selling for 17.9 cents per pound in 1929; in 1932, for 4.6 cents; the decline was nearly 75 percent.

Tobacco was selling for 17.3 cents per pound in 1929; in 1932, for 6.4 cents; the decline was more than 60 percent.

Hay was selling for $11.88 per ton in 1929; in 1932, for $7.60; the decline was more than 35 percent.

Hogs were selling for $9.80 per 100 pounds in 1929; in 1932, for $2.82; the decline was more than 70 percent.

Steers were selling for $9.72 per 100 pounds in 1929; in 1932, for $3.81; the decline was more than 60 per cent.

Such is the official record of prices on the farm, the figures shown being the average of all grades. In the face of a worldwide depression unchecked by political leadership, these declines probably were inevitable. It would be silly to charge them to the Federal Farm Board. They demonstrate, however, the utter inability of the "great instrumentality" to "assure" the "constructive action" which was the only reason for its existence. The whole cost of this ghastly experiment—the first of the Hoover Commissions—cannot be totted down now, but in a few years it will be apparent even to the dullest.

Thus fades the beautiful rainbow. As we near its end we find not the pot of gold but the usual gold brick.

The next outstanding Hoover Commission was the one headed by Mr. George W. Wickersham. So well known was this organization that its official title—The National Commission on Law Observance and Enforcement—was ignored and it became designated generally as the Wickersham Commission. The violent controversy that attended publication of its report simultaneous with President Hoover's virtual repudiation of its recommendations detracted much from the Commission's labors which were not confined to prohibition alone but included all law enforcement.

Months before Herbert Hoover took the oath as President, he let it be known that he would appoint the Commission. In December, 1928, Senator Glass of Virginia, anticipating the appointment, inserted a clause in a deficiency appropriation bill, providing $250,000 to defray the Commission's expenses. The clause remained in the bill when it was passed, so that money was available for the work before Mr. Hoover became President.

Apparently, Mr. Hoover overlooked this fund. The Commission was appointed May 20, 1929, and thirty days later, on June 19, Senator Glass, in addressing the Senate, spoke, in part, as follows:

"When the Commission was first appointed and assembled at the White House there was given out, through the Associated Press, this statement:

"'Since Congress has provided no funds, the Commissioners must serve without pay, at least at the start,

196

and their expenses will have to be taken care of out of the White House contingent fund until Congress can appropriate the necessary money. This probably will be done at the present session on the ground of an emergency situation requiring action.'

"That was not a random newspaper report. It was a statement authorized at the White House where apparently it was not known that the Congress had appropriated $250,000 for the purpose of a thorough inquiry into the problem of enforcing prohibition, and it required the President to report to Congress the result of such an investigation, together with his recommendations. The White House persisted in that statement until 12 o'clock noon of the following day when they were shown this provision of the deficiency Act of the last Congress."

Thus it would appear that the President, overlooking an essential detail, did not know of the existence of a fund to carry on the work at the time the Commission was appointed. Under such inauspicious circumstances did the second great Hoover Commission first fill its lungs.

The work of the Wickersham Commission is so recent and it received such a profusion of publicity that its review is not warranted here. The Commission itself wrought prodigiously in delving into conditions and laws, and its long report, issued in a continuing series of pamphlets, covered the whole range of law enforcement. But it led nowhere; the President responsible for its creation disagreed with certain of its prohibition conclusions and so advised Congress. Aside from the able report it rendered—and for their labor the members of the Commission received little thanks—the Commission accomplished nothing concrete in legislation. The money it spent produced no harvest of benefits.

The cost of the Wickersham Commission to the taxpayers, according to the Budget, was $244,452.51 in the fiscal year 1931, and $148,775.21 during the fiscal year 1930, a total of $393,227.72. No detailed accounting of the expenditure is given in the budget reports, nor is such accounting required by law. With headquarters in Washington, a modest staff and an unpretentious establishment, the Commission undoubtedly spent much of its funds in research and necessary travel.

Contrary to general belief, these two Commissions were the only Commissions appointed by Mr. Hoover which made any considerable drafts on the public treasury. Not that Mr. Hoover did not appoint other Commissions; he did so, rapidly, during the first half year of his Administration; and somewhat more slowly thereafter. But most of the Hoover Commissions were financed privately. It is reported at Washington that somewhat more than $2,000,000 was involved in the financing. No official figures, however, are available upon which to verify the accuracy of the report.

Both of the outstanding Hoover Commissions were what the users of street jargon call busts. The Wickersham Commission brought upon Washington such a rain of criticism as to astonish the sensitive occupant of the White House, and the Federal Farm Board failed dismally to accomplish its purpose. Government by Hoover Commissions, or so much of government as devolved upon those two Commissions, flunked.

During the first two years of his administration, Mr. Hoover appointed 32 Commissions, the great majority of which were financed privately. In its admirable report, "Presidential Commissions," *Editorial Research Reports* lists the Hoover Commissions during that period as follows:

1. Yellowstone National Park Boundary Commission—authorized by joint resolution of Congress, February 28, 1929.

2. Interoceanic Canal Board (Nicaraguan Canal Commission)—authorized by resolution of Congress, March 2, 1929.

3. National Memorial Commission (Negro)—created by joint resolution of Congress, March 4, 1929.

4. Interdepartmental Committee on Ocean Mail Contracts—appointed May, 1929.

5. National Commission on Law Observance and Enforcement—appointed May 20, 1929.

6. Veterans' Committee—appointed by letter May 23, 1929.

7. Federal Farm Board—created by act of Congress, June 15, 1929.

8. Commission to represent U. S. at celebration of

1,000th anniversary of the Althing of Iceland—authorized by joint resolution of Congress, June 21, 1929.

9. Conference on Child Health and Protection—appointed July 2, 1929.

10. San Francisco Bridge Commission—appointed September 25, 1929.

11. Advisory Committee on Illiteracy—appointed November 1, 1929.

12. Committee on the Conservation and Administration of the Public Domain—appointed November, 1929.

13. National Business Survey Conference—called at the direction of President Hoover by Julius Barnes, December 5, 1929.

14. Delegation to London Naval Conference—announced by State Department December 17, 1929.

15. Research Committee on Social Trends—appointed December 19, 1929.

16. Commission to Study and Review United States Policies in Haiti—appropriation authorized by joint resolution of Congress, Feb. 6, 1930.

17. The Battle of Monongahela Commission—created by joint resolution of Congress, April 21, 1930.

18. Committee relating to Chicago World's Fair Centennial Celebration—authorized by joint resolution of Congress, June 20, 1930.

19. Commission relating to International Exposition of Colonial and Overseas Countries, Paris, France—authorized by joint resolution of Congress, June 24, 1930.

20. U. S. Massachusetts Bay Colony Tercentenary

Commission—created by joint resolution of Congress, June 27, 1930.

21. Advisory Shipping Committee—appointed July, 1930.

22. Alaska Highway Commission—appointed July 28, 1930.

23. Conference on Home Building and Ownership —appointed August 1, 1930.

24. California Water Resources Commission—appointed to cooperate with state commission previously appointed by Governor Young, 1929-1930.

25. Advisory Committee on Employment Statistics —appointed August 12, 1930.

26. National Drought Committee — announced August 19, 1930.

27. Emergency Committee for Employment—announced October 17, 1930.

28. National Timber Conservation Board — appointed December 5, 1930.

29. Federal Power Commission (reorganization)— nominated December 3, 1930.

30. United States Tariff Commission (reorganization)—nominated December 3, 1930.

31. War Policies Commission—authorized by Congress in January, 1931.

32. Federal Employment Stabilization Board—authorized by Act of Congress, February 10, 1931.

There have been fewer Commissions appointed by the President thus far in the latter half of his administration. Perhaps he has sensed the public mistrust of them since the fiasco of the Wickersham report. The most notable, perhaps, of the few Commissions appointed more recently by the President is the Anti-Hoarding organization headed by Col. Frank Knox, Chicago publisher. Whatever the motive, the fact remains that the Commission habit has not the hold now upon the President that it had earlier in his official life.

The survey ends. Throughout it has been marked by poor guessing, ineptitude, waste and extravagance. The Commissions cited in detail failed to function to the high desire of their creator. The President's personal administration of the White House has been marked financially by an utter lack of the economy he imposed on his subordinates. House and Senate records tell of petty graft safely and comfortably legalized, and of disregard of public funds unworthy the trustees of those funds.

Something evidently is wrong at Washington. Is it fitting that the heavy taxes imposed on the harassed nation should go to buy political gold bricks or to further political bunk at ruinous prices? Where is the propriety of a President's spending more and more to maintain his personal establishment while $1,200 government clerks suffer from salary cuts? What possible justification exists for numerous senseless congressional junkets and investigations financed by levies wrung from poverty-stricken millions?

Senators, Representatives, how can you justify the mileage grab? Those weasel words, "It is the law," ring hollow in the knowledge that you made it the law. Do you, returning to those whose votes sent you to Washington in the first place, tell them how you pamper your personal love for little luxuries at the public expense? Do you tell them that you mail them Christmas cards at their expense? Do you tell them how you line up on opening day of the session to get that $125 in real cash for your stationery?

You bet you don't. You tell them none of these things. You speak of higher things than the abuse and misuse of your power to frank tommyrot through the mails at *their* expense. You soft-pedal the names on the government pay roll, so far as your offices are concerned, many of you. You say little of all these things and others.

But, really, isn't it time to abandon these things and to begin now to give full, unstinted return for every dollar coming to you from the public treasury?

It is. It is time to apply to the public business the same standards of integrity, decency and economy as you apply to your private affairs. In other words, the time is here —NOW—when we should get down to the level of 100 percent integrity and real economy in administering the public funds. God knows they come hard; let them go hard, too.

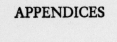

APPENDICES

Appendix A

Mileage Paid Senators

Senate Document No. 1 (Report of the Secretary of the Senate from July 1, 1930, to June 30, 1931) lists payments (beginning on Page 68) made on various dates as mileage to Senators for attending the special session of the Senate convened July 7, 1930. The payments are shown below, as disclosed by the official record.

In addition, unofficial figures are shown in each case to cover the round trip cost of transportation and a lower pullman berth from the Senator's home to Washington and return. Following those figures is shown, in each case, the excess charge upon the treasury. The excess, it should be borne in mind, is figured without regard to meals, tips and other incidental expenses during the trip.

Henry J. Allen of Kansas, $592.40 mileage, paid July 23, 1930. Actual cost of transportation from Wichita to Washington and return is $129.30. The excess is $463.10.

Henry F. Ashurst of Arizona, $1,050.40 mileage, paid October 9, 1930. Actual cost of transportation from Prescott to Washington and return is $234.28. The excess is $816.12.

Alben W. Barkley of Kentucky, $355.20 mileage, paid July 22, 1930. Actual cost of transportation from Paducah to Washington and return is $78.42. The excess is $276.78.

Hiram Bingham of Connecticut, $122.00 mileage, paid July 22, 1930. Actual cost of transportation from New Haven to Washington and return is $32.30. The excess is $89.70.

Hugo L. Black of Alabama, $305.20 mileage, paid July 22, 1930. Actual cost of transportation from Birmingham to Washington and return is $72.10. The excess is $233.10.

John J. Blaine of Wisconsin, $396 mileage, paid July 31, 1930. Actual cost of transportation from Boscobel to Washington and return is $92.98. The excess is $303.02.

Cole L. Blease of South Carolina, $208.80 mileage, paid September 20, 1930. Actual cost of transportation from Columbia to Washington and return is $45.58. The excess is $163.22.

William F. Borah of Idaho, $1,058.80 mileage, paid July 22, 1930. Actual cost of transportation from Boise to Washington and return is $239.56. The excess is $819.24.

Sam G. Bratton of New Mexico, $850.40 mileage, paid October 9, 1930. Actual cost of transportation from Albuquerque to Washington and return is $192.06. The excess is $658.34.

W. E. Brock of Tennessee, $248 mileage, paid July 22, 1930. Actual cost of transportation from Chattanooga to Washington and return is $58.04. The excess is $189.96.

Smith W. Brookhart of Iowa, $416 mileage, paid July 22, 1930. Actual cost of transportation from Washington, Iowa, to Washington, D. C., and return is $96.54. The excess is $319.46.

E. S. Broussard of Louisiana, $497.60 mileage, paid July 31, 1930. Actual cost of transportation from New Iberia to Washington and return is $120.66. The excess is $376.94.

Arthur Capper of Kansas, $494.40 mileage, paid July 22, 1930. Actual cost of transportation from Topeka to Washington and return is $114.68. The excess is $379.72.

Tom Connally of Texas, $740.80 mileage, paid August 18, 1930. Actual cost of transportation from Marlin to Washington and return is $137.06. The excess is $603.74.

Royal S. Copeland of New York, $94.00 mileage, paid July 22, 1930. Actual cost of transportation from Suffern to Washington and return is $26.08. The excess is $67.92.

James Couzens of Michigan, $244.00 mileage, paid July 22, 1930. Actual cost of transportation from Detroit to Washington and return is $55.86. The excess is $188.14.

Bronson Cutting of New Mexico, $834 mileage, paid October 10, 1930. Actual cost of transportation from Santa Fé to Washington and return is $189.78. The excess is $644.22.

Porter H. Dale of Vermont, $246 mileage, paid August 7, 1930. Actual cost of transportation from Island Pond to Washington and return is $64.48. The excess is $181.52.

Charles S. Deneen of Illinois, $316.00 mileage, paid July 22, 1930. Actual cost of transportation from Chicago to Washington and return is $72.06. The excess is $243.94.

Simeon D. Fess of Ohio, $249.20 mileage, paid July 22, 1930. Actual cost of transportation from Yellow Springs to Washington and return is $50.78. The excess is $198.42.

Duncan U. Fletcher of Florida, $306.80 mileage, paid July 22, 1930. Actual cost of transportation from Jacksonville to Washington and return is $74.08. The excess is $232.72.

Lynn J. Frazier of North Dakota, $638 mileage, paid October 9, 1930. Actual cost of transportation from Hoople to Washington and return is $142.44. The excess is $495.56.

Walter F. George of Georgia, $301.20 mileage, paid July 22, 1930. Actual cost of transportation from Vienna to Washington and return is $68.36. The excess is $232.84.

F. H. Gillett of Massachusetts, $145.60 mileage, paid July 22, 1930. Actual cost of transportation from Westfield to Washington and return is $39.72. The excess is $105.88.

Carter Glass of Virginia, $69.60 mileage, paid July 26, 1930. Actual cost of transportation from Lynchburg to Washington and return is $19.20. The excess is $50.40.

Otis F. Glenn of Illinois, $324 mileage, paid July 22, 1930. Actual cost of transportation from Murphysboro to Washington and return is $82.86. The excess is $241.14.

P. L. Goldsborough of Maryland, $16 mileage, paid July 22, 1930. Actual cost of transportation from Baltimore to Washington and return is $4.38. The excess is $11.62.

Guy D. Goff of West Virginia, $110.40 mileage, paid August 20, 1930. Actual cost of transportation from Clarksburg to Washington and return is $27.40. The excess is $83.

A. R. Gould of Maine, $361.20 mileage, paid July 22, 1930. Actual cost of transportation from Presque Isle to Washington and return is $79.48. The excess is $281.72.

Joseph R. Grundy of Pennsylvania, $64.80 mileage, paid December 3, 1930. Actual cost of transportation from Bristol to Washington and return is $18.54. The excess is $46.26.

Frederick Hale of Maine, $227.20 mileage, paid July 22, 1930. Actual cost of transportation from Portland to Washington and return is $54.88. The excess is $172.32.

Pat Harrison of Mississippi, $430 mileage, paid July 22, 1930. Actual cost of transportation from Gulfport to Washington and return is $99.16. The excess is $330.84.

Daniel O. Hastings of Delaware, $43.60 mileage, paid July 31, 1930. Actual cost of transportation from Wilmington to Washington and return (including parlor car seat instead of lower berth, as the trip required but little more than two hours) is $9.38. The excess is $34.22.

H. D. Hatfield of West Virginia, $173.20 mileage, paid July 22, 1930. Actual cost of transportation from Huntington to Washington and return is $40.36. The excess is $132.84.

Harry B. Hawes, of Missouri, $356.80 mileage, paid July 26, 1930. Actual cost of transportation from St. Louis to Washington and return is $83.08. The excess is $273.72.

Carl Hayden of Arizona, $1,108.40 mileage, paid August 15, 1930. Actual cost of transportation from Phoenix to Washington and return is $234.28. The excess is $874.12.

Felix Hebert of Rhode Island, $170.80 mileage, paid July 22, 1930. Actual cost of transportation from West Warwick to Washington and return is $43.56. The excess is $127.24.

J. Thomas Heflin of Alabama, $310 mileage, paid July 31, 1930. Actual cost of transportation from Lafayette to Washington and return is $72.12. The excess is $237.88.

R. B. Howell of Nebraska, $524.80 mileage, paid July 22, 1930. Actual cost of transportation from Omaha to Washington and return is $115.42. The excess is $409.38.

Hiram W. Johnson of California, $1,292.80 mileage, paid July 22, 1930. Actual cost of transportation from San Francisco to Washington and return is $274.76. The excess is $1,018.04.

Wesley L. Jones of Washington, $1,347.20 mileage, paid July 22, 1930. Actual cost of transportation from Seattle to Washington and return is $272.98. The excess is $1,074.22.

Hamilton F. Kean of New Jersey, $92 mileage, paid July 22, 1930. Actual cost of transportation from Elizabeth to Washington and return is $22.86. The excess is $69.14.

John B. Kendrick of Wyoming, $808.40 mileage, paid July 22, 1930. Actual cost of transportation from Sheridan to Washington and return is $180.30. The excess is $628.10.

Henry W. Keyes of New Hampshire, $253.20 mileage, paid July 22, 1930. Actual cost of transportation from North Haverhill to Washington and return is $48.24. The excess is $204.96.

William H. King of Utah, $960 mileage, paid July 25, 1930. Actual cost of transportation from Salt Lake City to Washington and return is $212.96. The excess is $747.04.

Robert M. LaFollette of Wisconsin, $371.60 mileage, paid July 22, 1930. Actual cost of transportation from Madison to Washington and return is $82.92. The excess is $288.68.

Roscoe C. McCulloch of Ohio, $216.00 mileage, paid July 22, 1930. Actual cost of transportation from Canton to Washington and return is $38.12. The excess is $177.88.

Kenneth McKellar of Tennessee, $372.80 mileage, paid July 22, 1930. Actual cost of transportation from Memphis to Washington and return is $87.40. The excess is $285.40.

W. H. McMaster of South Dakota, $542.40 mileage, paid July 31, 1930. Actual cost of transportation from Yankton to Washington and return is $123.70. The excess is $418.70.

Charles L. McNary of Oregon, $1,266 mileage, paid July 22, 1930. Actual cost of transportation from Salem to Washington and return is $276.80. The excess is $989.20.

Jesse H. Metcalf of Rhode Island, $166 mileage, paid July 22, 1930. Actual cost of transportation from Providence to Washington and return is $42.70. The excess is $123.30.

George H. Moses of New Hampshire, $216.40 mileage, paid July 22, 1930. Actual cost of transportation from Concord to Washington and return is $51.14. The excess is $165.26.

Peter Norbeck of South Dakota, $587.20 mileage, paid September 12, 1930. Actual cost of transportation from Redfield to Washington and return is $133.18. The excess is $454.02.

Gerald P. Nye of North Dakota, $630 mileage, paid August 2, 1930. Actual cost of transportation from Cooperstown to Washington and return is $139. The excess is $491.

Tasker L. Oddie of Nevada, $1,125.60 mileage, paid July 22, 1930. Actual cost of transportation from Reno to Washington and return is $260.88. The excess is $864.72.

Roscoe C. Patterson of Missouri, $516 mileage, paid July 22, 1930. Actual cost of transportation from Kansas City to Washington and return is $109.16. The excess is $406.84.

Lawrence C. Phipps of Colorado, $748.40 mileage, paid July 22, 1930. Actual cost of transportation from Denver to Washington and return is $166.12. The excess is $582.28.

W. B. Pine of Oklahoma, $544 mileage, paid July 22, 1930. Actual cost of transportation from Okmulgee to Washington and return is $126.34. The excess is $417.66.

Key Pittman of Nevada, $1,277.20 mileage, paid July 22, 1930. Actual cost of transportation from Tonopah to Washington and return is $281.40. The excess is $995.80.

Joseph E. Ransdell of Louisiana, $440.40 mileage, paid August 16, 1930. Actual cost of transportation from Lake Providence to Washington and return is $111.40. The excess is $329.

David A. Reed of Pennsylvania, $120.80 mileage, paid July 22, 1930. Actual cost of transportation from Pittsburgh to Washington and return is $29.30. The excess is $91.50.

Joe T. Robinson of Arkansas, $536.40 mileage, paid July 22, 1930. Actual cost of transportation from Little Rock to Washington and return is $99.58. The excess is $436.82.

A. R. Robinson of Indiana, $296 mileage, paid July 22, 1930. Actual cost of transportation from Indianapolis to Washington and return is $63.20. The excess is $232.80.

J. M. Robsion of Kentucky, $255.20 mileage, paid July 22, 1930. Actual cost of transportation from Barbourville to Washington and return is $59.04. The excess is $196.16.

Thomas D. Schall of Minnesota, $512.40 mileage, paid July 31, 1930. Actual cost of transportation from Minneapolis to Washington and return is $108.88. The excess is $403.52.

Morris Sheppard of Texas, $483.60 mileage, paid July 22, 1930. Actual cost of transportation from Texarkana to Washington and return is $116.76. The excess is $366.84.

Henrik Shipstead of Minnesota, $478 mileage, paid July 23, 1930. Actual cost of transportation from Minneapolis to Washington and return is $108.88. The excess is $369.12.

Samuel M. Shortridge of California, $1,304.40 mileage paid July 22, 1930. Actual cost of transportation from Menlo Park to Washington and return is $274.76. The excess is $1,029.64.

E. D. Smith of South Carolina, $176 mileage, paid July 26, 1930. Actual cost of transportation from Lynchburg to Washington and return is $40.08. The excess is $135.92.

Reed Smoot of Utah, $978 mileage, paid July 22, 1930. Actual cost of transportation from Provo to Washington and return is $212.96. The excess is $765.04.

Daniel F. Steck of Iowa, $426 mileage, paid July 31, 1930. Actual cost of transportation from Ottumwa to Washington and return is $99.72. The excess is $326.28.

Frederick Steiwer of Oregon, $1,245.20 mileage, paid July 24, 1930. Actual cost of transportation from Portland to Washington and return is $272.98. The excess is $972.22.

Hubert D. Stephens of Mississippi, $361.20 mileage, paid July 31, 1930. Actual cost of transportation from New Albany to Washington and return is $93.16. The excess is $268.04.

Patrick Sullivan of Wyoming, $785.60 mileage, paid July 22, 1930. Actual cost of transportation from Casper to Washington and return is $172.56. The excess is $613.04.

Claude A. Swanson of Virginia, $89.20 mileage, paid July 26, 1930. Actual cost of transportation from Chatham to Washington and return is $23.22. The excess is $65.98.

John Thomas of Idaho, $1,028.80 mileage, paid August 5, 1930. Actual cost of transportation from Gooding to Washington and return is $219.64. The excess is $809.16.

Elmer Thomas of Oklahoma, $650.80 mileage, paid July 22, 1930. Actual cost of transportation from Medicine Park to Washington and return is $142.12. The excess is $508.68.

J. G. Townsend of Delaware, $86.40 mileage, paid July 26, 1930. Actual cost of transportation from Selbyville to Washington and return is $23.06. The excess is $63.34.

Park Trammell of Florida, $391.60 mileage, paid July 22, 1930. Actual cost of transportation from Lakeland to Washington and return is $93. The excess is $298.60.

A. H. Vandenberg of Michigan, $308 mileage, paid July 22, 1930. Actual cost of transportation from Grand Rapids to Washington and return is $63.66. The excess is $244.34.

Robert F. Wagner of New York, $96 mileage, paid July 22, 1930. Actual cost of transportation from New York to Washington and return is $23.78. The excess is $72.22.

F. C. Walcott of Connecticut, $139.60 mileage, paid July 22, 1930. Actual cost of transportation from Norfolk to Washington and return is $32.18. The excess is $107.42.

David I. Walsh of Massachusetts, $203.60 mileage, paid July 22, 1930. Actual cost of transportation from Clinton to Washington and return is $38.60. The excess is $165.

Thomas J. Walsh of Montana, $951.20 mileage, paid July 22, 1930. Actual cost of transportation from Helena to Washington and return is $210.72. The excess is $740.48.

Charles W. Waterman of Colorado, $748 mileage, paid July 26, 1930. Actual cost of transportation from Denver to Washington and return is $166.12. The excess is $581.88.

James E. Watson of Indiana, $255.20 mileage, paid July 22, 1930. Actual cost of transportation from Rushville to Washington and return is $58.52. The excess is $196.68.

Burton K. Wheeler of Montana, $946 mileage, paid December 3, 1930. Actual cost of transportation from Butte to Washington and return is $210.72. The excess is $735.28.

Appendix B

Payments for Stationery

As related in Chapter IX, Representatives are allowed $125 apiece to cover stationery and office supplies with which to conduct their official correspondence. Many Representatives prefer the cash to the stationery. Others take part cash and part stationery. A few find the $125 insufficient; these make up the difference from their own pockets.

House Document No. 2 lists the Representatives who received cash in the fiscal year 1931. There are 230 names on the list. It follows, together the dates on which payments were made. Unless otherwise noted, the payments cover the fiscal year 1931. Dozens of Representatives, it will be noted, allowed their credits to accumulate over two or more years and withdrew the full amount in 1931. Senators receiving cash on their stationery allowance are listed in Chapter IX. The Representatives follow:

Aldrich, Richard S., of Rhode Island. Paid $125 December 6, 1930.

Allen, John C., of Illinois. Paid $125 December 12, 1930.

Almon, Edward B., of Alabama. Paid $88.03 March 9, 1931.

Arentz, Samuel S., of Nevada. Paid $50.17 April 9, 1931.

Aswell, James B., of Louisiana. Paid $125 March 12, 1931.

Ayres, W. A., of Kansas. Paid $107.25 December 3, 1930.

Baird, Joe E., of Ohio. Paid $125 March 3, 1931. Also, on the same date, $104.79 to cover accumulated credits in 1930. Total payment, $229.79.

Bankhead, William B., of Alabama. Paid $70.80 February 28, 1931.

Barbour, Henry E., of California. Paid $61.07 March 20, 1931. Also, on July 3, 1930, paid $110.86 to cover accumulated credits during 1930. Total payments, $171.93.

Beers, Edward M., of Pennsylvania. Paid $125 December 15, 1930.

Black, Loring M., of New York. Paid $114.44 December 23, 1930.

Blackburn, Robert, of Kentucky. Paid $125 January 22, 1931. Also, on the same date, paid $2.96 to cover accumulated credits during 1930. Total payment, $127.96.

Bland, Schuyler Otis, of Virginia. Paid $125 December 15, 1930.

Bohn, Frank P., of Michigan. Paid $113.84 March 5, 1931. Also, on December 9, 1930, paid $58.61 to cover accumulated credits in 1930. Total payments, $172.45.

Box, John C., of Texas. Paid $125 March 3, 1931. Also, on the same date, paid $31.75 to cover accumulated credits for 1929-30. Total payment, $156.75.

Boylan, John J., of New York. Paid $88.50 August 11, 1930, to cover accumulated credits for 1930.

Brand, Charles H., of Georgia. Paid $111.05 December 2, 1930.

Briggs, Clay Stone, of Texas. Paid $116.97 July 14, 1930, to cover accumulated credits for 1930.

Brigham, Elbert S., of Vermont. Paid $125 March 6, 1931. Also on the same date paid $125 to cover accumulated credits for 1930, and $11.57 for 1929. Total payment, $261.57.

Browne, Edward E., of Wisconsin. Paid $90.54 February 21, 1931. Also, on July 29, 1930, paid $74.32 to cover accumulated credits for 1930. Total payments, $164.86.

Browning, Gordon, of Tennessee. Paid $125 January 6, 1931.

Brumm, George F., of Pennsylvania. Paid $84.87 January 30, 1931.

Burdick, Clark, of Rhode Island. Paid $64.79 March 26, 1931.

Burtness, Olger B., of North Dakota. Paid $125 March 26, 1931.

Busby, Jeff, of Mississippi. Paid $116.78 December 15, 1930.

Butler, Robert R., of Oregon. Paid $125 April 13, 1931. Also, on the same date, paid $125 to cover accumulated credits for 1930. Total payment, $250.

Byrns, Joseph W., of Tennessee. Paid $125 March 11, 1931. Also, on the same date, paid $125 to cover accumulated credits for 1930. Total payment, $250.

Cable, John L., of Ohio. Paid $76.79 November 14, 1930.

Campbell, Guy E., of Pennsylvania. Paid $100.63 December 9, 1930.

Canfield, Harry C., of Indiana. Paid $125 December 20, 1930.

Chalmers, W. W., of Ohio. Paid $125 December 3, 1930.

Chase, J. Mitchell, of Pennsylvania. Paid $65.62 December 15, 1930.

Chindblom, Carl R., of Illinois. Paid $125 March 12, 1931.

Clancy, Robert H., of Michigan. Paid $121.92 December 4, 1930.

Clark, Linwood L., of Maryland. Paid $93.91 February 13, 1931. Also, on July 10, 1930, paid $109.35 to cover accumulated credits for 1930. Total payments, $203.26.

Collier, James W., of Mississippi. Paid $94.53 December 3, 1930.

Colton, Don B., of Utah. Paid $109.07 December 20, 1930.

Connery, William P., of Massachusetts. Paid $106.22 February 25, 1931.

Connolly, James J., of Pennsylvania. Paid $125 December 13, 1930.

Cooper, Henry Allen, of Wisconsin. Paid $92.38 December 18, 1930.

Cooper, Jere, of Tennessee. Paid $125 March 5, 1931.

Cooper, John G., of Ohio. Paid $80.01 February 23, 1931.

Cox, E. E., of Georgia. Paid $125 December 19, 1930.

Craddock, J. D., of Kentucky. Paid $72.44 February 26, 1931.

Cramton, Louis C., of Michigan. Paid $125 January 3, 1931. Also, on March 28, 1931, paid $28.05 to cover accumulated credits for 1930. Total payments, $153.05.

Crisp, Charles R., of Georgia. Paid $125 December 16, 1930.

Crowther, Frank, of New York. Paid $121.97 March 26, 1931.

Dallinger, Frederick W., of Massachusetts. Paid $81.88 January 6, 1931, to cover accumulated credits for 1930.

Darrow, George P., of Pennsylvania. Paid $106.75 March 6, 1931.

Davila, F. C., Porto Rican Commissioner. Paid $76.14 March 9, 1931. Also, on July 1, 1930, paid $81.92 to cover accumulated credits for 1930. Total payments, $158.06.

Davis, Ewin L., of Tennessee. Paid $73.25 March 2, 1931. Also, on July 1, 1930, paid $71.44 to cover accumulated credits for 1930. Total payments, $144.69.

Dempsey, S. Wallace, of New York. Paid $125 February 27, 1931. Also, on the same date, paid $30.43 to cover accumulated credits for 1929. Total payments $155.43.

Denison, Edward E., of Illinois. Paid $125 December 9, 1930.

De Rouen, Rene, of Louisiana. Paid $112.80 December 13, 1930.

Dickinson, L. J., of Iowa. Paid $86.68 March 10, 1931.

Doughton, Robert L., of North Carolina. Paid $125 December 4, 1930.

Dowell, Cassius C., of Iowa. Paid $125 December 2, 1930.

Doyle, Thomas A., of Illinois. Paid $66.22 March 3, 1931.

Drewry, Patrick H., of Virginia. Paid $109.88 March 3, 1931.

Driver, William J., of Arkansas. Paid $25.79 December 2, 1930, to cover accumulated credits in 1930.

Dunbar, James W., of Indiana. Paid $56.04 July 10, 1930, to cover accumulated credits for 1930.

Edwards, Charles G., of Georgia. Paid $117.82 December 12, 1930.

Elliott, Richard N., of Indiana. Paid $120.35 March 2, 1931.

Ellis, Edgar C., of Missouri. Paid $87.92 January 7, 1931.

Evans, John M., of Montana. Paid $108.09 July 3, 1930, to cover accumulated credits for 1930.

Fenn, E. Hart, of Connecticut. Paid $64.47 March 5, 1931.

Fisher, Hubert F., of Tennessee. Paid $125 January 24, 1931. Also, on the same date, paid $86.42 to cover accumulated credits for 1929. Total payment, $211.42.

Fort, Franklin W., of New Jersey. Paid $125 February 20, 1931. Also, on the same date, paid $125 to cover accumulated credits for 1930, $125 for 1929 credits, and $38.09 for 1928 credits. Total payment, $413.09.

Frear, James A., of Wisconsin. Paid $125 May 19, 1931.

French, Burton L., of Idaho. Paid $117.46 December 2, 1930.

Fulmer, Hampton P., of South Carolina. Paid $95.45 January 26, 1931. Also, on July 3, 1930, paid $42.61 to cover accumulated credits for 1930. Total payments, $138.06.

Garner, John N., of Texas. Paid $125 December 4, 1930.

Gifford, Charles L., of Massachusetts. Paid $91.19 February 13, 1931.

Glover, D. D., of Arkansas. Paid $125 December 15, 1930. Also, on the same date, paid $107.39 to cover accumulated credits for 1930. Total payment, $232.39.

Graham, George S., of Pennsylvania. Paid $125 December 10, 1930, to cover accumulated credits for 1929-30. Also, on the same date, $375 to cover accumulated credits for 1929, 1928 and 1927. Total payment, $500.

Gregory, W. V., of Kentucky. Paid $69.92 December 9, 1930, to cover accumulated credits for 1930.

Hall, Albert R., of Indiana. Paid $93.14 February 27, 1931.

Hall, Homer W., of Illinois. Paid $125 February 17, 1931.

Halsey, Thomas J., of Missouri. Paid $125 February 2, 1931. Also, on the same date, paid $125 to cover accumulated credits for 1930. Total payment, $250.

Hardy, Guy U., of Colorado. Paid $67 November 28, 1930, to cover accumulated credits for 1930.

Hastings, William W., of Oklahoma. Paid $110.62 February 27, 1931.

Haugen, Gilbert N., of Iowa. Paid $125 January 9, 1931.

Hawley, Willis C., of Oregon. Paid $125 March 17, 1931. Also, on the same date, paid $124.49 to cover accumulated credits for 1930. Total payment, $249.49.

Hickey, Andrew J., of Indiana. Paid $116.42 March 3, 1931.

Hill, Lister, of Alabama. Paid $125 April 10, 1931. Also, on the same date, $125 to cover accumulated credits for 1930. Total payment, $250.

Hill, Sam B., of Washington. Paid $125 December 24, 1930. Also, on the same date, paid $125 to cover accumulated credits for 1930. Total payment, $250.

Hoch, Homer, of Kansas. Paid $82.22 March 5, 1931. Also, on July 3, 1930, paid $59.26 to cover accumulated credits for 1930. Total payments, $141.48.

Holaday, William P., of Illinois. Paid $75.90 February 23, 1931.

Howard, Edgar, of Nebraska. Paid $250 December 2, 1930, to cover accumulated credits for 1930 and 1929. Also, on the same date $76.13 to cover accumulated credits for 1928. Total payment, $326.13.

Huddleston, George, of Alabama. Paid $125 December 4, 1930.

Hudspeth, C. B., of Texas. Paid $123.09 February 7, 1931. Also, on January 26, 1931, $125 to cover accumulated credits for 1930. Total payments, $248.09.

Hudson, Grant M., of Michigan. Paid $100.71 March 3, 1931. Also, on July 1, 1930, paid $61.46 to cover accumulated credits for 1930. Total payments, $162.17.

Hull, Cordell, of Tennessee. Paid $305.52 March 5, 1931, to cover accumulated credits for 1931, 1930, and 1929.

Igoe, James T., of Illinois. Paid $125 December 4, 1930. Also, on March 2, 1931, paid $63.52 to cover accumulated credits for 1930. Total payments, $188.52.

Irwin, Ed. M., of Illinois. Paid $125 March 3, 1931. Also, on the same date, $466.96 to cover accumulated credits for 1930, 1929, 1928 and 1927. Total payment, $591.96.

Jenkins, Thomas A., of Ohio. Paid $75.78 March 6, 1931.

Johnson, Albert, of Washington. Paid $57.16 February 27, 1931.

Johnson, Fred G., of Nebraska. Paid $94.80 March 5, 1931.

Johnson, Jed, of Oklahoma. Paid $125 January 20, 1931.

Johnson, Luther A., of Texas. Paid $79.62 July 31, 1930, to cover accumulated credits for 1930.

Johnson, Noble J., of Indiana. Paid $125 March 5, 1931. Also, on the same date, $210.91 to cover accumulated credits for 1930 and 1929. Total payment, $335.91.

Johnson, Rowland J., of Missouri. Paid $119.38 February 25, 1931.

Johnson, Royal C., of South Dakota. Paid $125 January 3, 1931.

Jonas, Charles A., of North Carolina. Paid $57.85 December 6, 1930.

Jones, Marvin, of Texas. Paid $125 December 9, 1930.

Kahn, Florence P., of California. Paid $125 March 9, 1931. Also, on the same date, $3.41 to cover accumulated credits for 1928. Total payment, $128.41.

Kearns, Charles C., of Ohio. Paid $125 December 20, 1930. Also, on the same date, $341.88 to cover accumulated credits for 1930, 1929 and 1928. Total payment, $466.88.

Kendall, Elva R., of Kentucky. Paid $22.75 March 3, 1931.

Kendall, Samuel A., of Pennsylvania. Paid $125 March 9, 1931.

Kennedy, Martin J., of New York. Paid $78.79 December 19, 1930.

Kerr, John H., of North Carolina. Paid $88.75 December 6, 1930.

Ketcham, John C., of Michigan. Paid $74.93 November 28, 1930, to cover accumulated credits for 1930.

Kiefner, Charles E., of Missouri. Paid $125 February 27, 1931. Also, February 19, 1931, $51.90 to cover accumulated credits for 1930. Total payments, $176.90.

Kopp, William F., of Iowa. Paid $54.35 January 21, 1931.

Kunz, Stanley H., of Illinois. Paid $94.64 December 13, 1930.

Lambertson, W. P., of Kansas. Paid $125 December 3, 1930.

Lampert, Mary C., widow of Florian Lampert, of Wisconsin. Paid $39.03 November 3, 1930, to cover accumulated credits for 1930.

Langley, Katherine, of Kentucky. Paid $19.66 December 10, 1930.

Lanham, Fritz G., of Texas. Paid $125 December 2, 1930.

Lankford, Menalcus, of Virginia. Paid $74.63 March 12, 1931. Also, on July 31, 1930, paid $116.23 to cover accumulated credits for 1930. Total payments, $190.86.

Lankford, William G., of Georgia. Paid $95.40 December 2, 1931.

Lea, Clarence F., of California. Paid $125 July 11, 1930, to cover accumulated credits for 1930.

Lehlbach, Frederick R., of New Jersey. Paid $125 December 11, 1930, to cover accumulated credits for 1930.

Letts, F. Dickinson, of Iowa. Paid $125 February 26, 1931. Also, on the same date, paid $20.27 to cover accumulated credits for 1930. Total payment, $145.27.

Lindsay, George W., of New York. Paid $93.36 January 16, 1931.

Linthicum, J. Charles, of Maryland. Paid $125 December 12, 1930.

Longworth, Alice Roosevelt, widow of Nicholas Longworth, of Ohio. Paid $125 May 11, 1931. Also, on the same date, paid $139.41 to cover accumulated credits for 1930 and 1929. Total payment, $264.41.

Loofbourow, Frederick C., of Utah. Paid $47.64 March 3, 1931.

McFadden, Louis R., of Pennsylvania. Paid $125 April 10, 1931. Also, on the same date, $6.69 to cover accumulated credits for 1929. Total payment, $131.69.

McKeown, Tom D., of Oklahoma. Paid $102.57 February 26, 1931.

McLaughlin, James C., of Michigan. Paid $125 December 4, 1930.

McLeod, Clarence J., of Michigan. Paid $77.17 March 6, 1931.

McMillan, Thomas S., of South Carolina. Paid $106.81 December 9, 1930.

Menges, Franklin, of Pennsylvania. Paid $125 December 20, 1930. Also, on the same date, $320.25 paid to cover accumulated credits for 1930, 1929 and 1928. Total payment, $445.25.

Merritt, Schuyler, of Connecticut. Paid $125 February 27, 1931. Also, on the same date, $40.93 paid to cover accumulated credits for 1930. Total payment, $165.93.

Michaelson, M. Alfred, of Illinois. Paid $125 December 12, 1930. Also, on the same date, $27.28 to cover accumulated credits for 1930. Total payment, $152.28.

Miller, John F., of Washington. Paid $104.25 February 23, 1931.

Milligan, Jacob L., of Missouri. Paid $87.09 December 24, 1930.

Montague, Andrew J., of Virginia. Paid $72.58 July 1, 1930, to cover accumulated credits for 1930.

Montet, Numa F., of Louisiana. Paid $118.05 December 3, 1930.

Moore, C. Ellis, of Ohio. Paid $125 February 7, 1931.

Moore, John W., of Kentucky. Paid $99.64 January 7, 1931.

Moore, R. Walton, of Virginia. Paid $125 January 7, 1931. Also, on the same date, $107.99 paid to cover accumulated credits for 1930. Total payment, $232.99.

Morehead, John H., of Nebraska. Paid $125 December 30, 1930.

Morgan, William M., of Ohio. Paid $107.70 March 3, 1931.

Mouser, Grant E., of Ohio. Paid $67.66 December 11, 1930.

Nelson, John E., of Wisconsin. Paid $125 December 13, 1930.

Newhall, J. Lincoln, of Kentucky. Paid $125 March 2, 1931.

Niedringhaus, Henry F., of Missouri. Paid $118.13 February 25, 1931.

O'Connell, Mary Agnes, widow of D. J. O'Connell, of New York. Paid $125 January 13, 1931. Also, on the same date, $5.01 paid to cover accumulated credits for 1928. Total payment, $130.01.

O'Connor, Charles, of Oklahoma. Paid $45.78 March 5, 1931.

O'Connor, James, of Louisiana. Paid $125 December 11, 1930.

Oldfield, Pearl P., of Arkansas. Paid $125 December 9, 1930. Also, on the same date, paid $125 to cover accumulated credits for 1930. Total payment, $250.

Oliver, Frank, of New York. Paid $122.62 January 8, 1931. Also, December 19, 1930, paid $114.52 to cover accumulated credits for 1930. Total payment, $237.14.

Palmer, John W., of Missouri. Paid $125 February 21, 1931.

Palmisano, Vincent L., of Maryland. Paid $107.73 March 9, 1931.

Parks, Tilman B., of Arkansas. Paid $110.81 December 11, 1930.

Patman, Wright, of Texas. Paid $125 February 20, 1931.

Peavey, Hubert H., of Wisconsin. Paid $56.04 March 3, 1931.

Pou, Edward W., of North Carolina. Paid $110.61 March 6, 1931.

Prall, Anning S., of New York. Paid $87.43 March 26, 1931. Also, July 31, 1930, paid $28.01 to cover accumulated credits for 1930. Total payments, $115.44.

Pratt, Harcourt J., of New York. Paid $314.46 December 9, 1930, to cover accumulated credits for 1930, 1929 and 1928.

Pritchard, George H., of North Carolina. Paid $70.30 March 9, 1931.

Quin, Percy E., of Mississippi. Paid $94 December 19, 1930.

Ragon, Heartsill, of Arkansas. Paid $193.59 December 3, 1930, to cover accumulated credits for 1930 and 1929.

Ramey, Frank M., of Illinois. Paid $125 February 23, 1931. Also, on the same date, paid $94.50 to cover accumulated credits in 1930. Total payment, $219.50.

Ramseyer, C. W., of Iowa. Paid $125 June 23, 1931. Also, on the same date, $125 paid to cover credits accumulated for 1930. Total payment, $250.

Rankin, John E., of Mississippi. Paid $125 December 20, 1930.

Rayburn, Sam, of Texas. Paid $125 December 9, 1930.

Romjue, Milton A., of Missouri. Paid $125 January 13, 1931.

Rowbottom, Harry E., of Indiana. Paid $125 February 4, 1931. Also, on the same date, $94.31 paid to cover accumulated credits for 1930. Total payment, $219.31.

Rutherford, Samuel, of Georgia. Paid $73.92 March 5, 1931. Also, July 1, 1930, paid $32.12 to cover accumulated credits for 1930. Total payments, $106.04.

Sabath, A. J., of Illinois. Paid $125 March 3, 1931. Also,

on the same date, $84.05 paid to cover accumulated credits for 1930. Total payments, $209.05.

Sanders, Archie D., of New York. Paid $125 March 5, 1931.

Sanders, Morgan G., of Texas. Paid $104.90 December 19, 1930.

Sandlin, John N., of Louisiana. Paid $125 December 3, 1930.

Sears, Willis G., of Nebraska. Paid $124 February 4, 1931.

Segar, George N., of New Jersey. Paid $125 October 16, 1930, to cover accumulated credits for 1929-30.

Selvig, Conrad G., of Minnesota. Paid $109.61 December 4, 1930.

Shaffer, Joseph C., of Virginia. Paid $125 February 17, 1931. Also, on the same date, $156.91 paid to cover accumulated credits for 1930 and 1929. Total payment, $281.91.

Short, Dewey, of Missouri. Paid $125 March 5, 1931. Also, on the same date, $148.74 paid to cover accumulated credits for 1930 and 1929. Total payment, $273.74.

Shreve, Milton W., of Pennsylvania. Paid $105.32 December 2, 1930.

Simms, Albert Gallatin, of New Mexico. Paid $61.37 March 3, 1931.

Sloan, Charles, of Nebraska. Paid $80.55 March 5, 1931.

Smart, Walter P., executor of the estate of S. G. Porter of Pennsylvania. Paid $412.06 January 6, 1931, to cover accumulated credits for 1931, 1930, 1929 and 1928.

Smith, Addison, of Idaho. Paid $103.56 December 3, 1930.

Smith, Joe L., of West Virginia. Paid $125 March 3, 1931.

Snell, Bertrand H., of New York. Paid $125 February 16, 1931. Also, on the same date, $170.02 paid to cover accumulated credits for 1930 and 1929. Total payment, $295.02.

Sparks, Charles I., of Kansas. Paid $125 December 19, 1930.

Speaks, John C., of Ohio. Paid $35.92 March 3, 1931. Also, July 3, 1930, paid $87.19 to cover accumulated credits for 1930. Total payments, $123.11.

Spearing, J. Zach., of Louisiana. Paid $125 December 6, 1930.

Sproul, Elliott W., of Illinois. Paid $125 February 26, 1931. Also, on the same date, $180.12 paid to cover accumulated credits for 1930 and 1929. Total payment, $305.12.

Sproul, W. H., of Kansas. Paid $123.86 March 5, 1931.

Stalker, Gale H., of New York. Paid $125 December 10, 1930.

Steagall, Henry B., of Alabama. Paid $94.55 December 3, 1930.

Stevenson, William F., of Pennsylvania. Paid $125 December 2, 1931.

Stobbs, George R., of Massachusetts. Paid $125 March 3, 1931. Also, on the same date, $54.49 paid to cover accumulated credits for 1929-30. Total payment, $179.49.

Stone, U. S., of Oklahoma. Paid $83.34 February 4, 1931.

Strong, James G., of Kansas. Paid $125 December 4, 1930.

Strong, Nathan L., of Pennsylvania. Paid $98.53 December 20, 1930.

Sullivan, Patrick J., of Pennsylvania. Paid $98.71 October 3, 1930, to cover accumulated credits in 1930.

Sumners, Hatton W., of Texas. Paid $125 December 6, 1931.

Sutherland, Dan, Delegate from Alaska. Paid $91.16 March 2, 1931. Also, on September 12, 1930, paid $160.35 to cover accumulated credits for 1930 and 1929. Total payments, $251.51.

Swanson, Charles E., of Iowa. Paid $125 July 24, 1930, to cover accumulated credits for 1930.

Swick, J. Howard, of Pennsylvania. Paid $125 July 3, 1930, to cover accumulated credits for 1930.

Swing, Philip D., of California. Paid $105.23 December 27, 1930.

Taylor, Edward T., of Colorado. Paid $98.15 April 20, 1931. Also, on July 3, 1930, paid $250 to cover accumulated credits for 1930 and 1929. Total payments, $348.15.

Taylor, J. Will, of Tennessee. Paid $109.14 March 5, 1931.

Temple, Henry W., of Pennsylvania. Paid $125 December 2, 1930.

Thatcher, Maurice H., of Kentucky. Paid $125 July 18, 1930, to cover accumulated credits for 1930.

Thompson, Charles J., of Ohio. Paid $111.91 December 4, 1930.

Tilson, John Q., of Connecticut. Paid $121.30 February 20, 1931.

Treadway, Allen T., of Massachusetts. Paid $125 December 2, 1930, to cover accumulated credits for 1930. Also, December 4, 1930, paid $234.98 to cover accumulated credits for 1929 and 1928. Total payments, $359.98.

Tucker, H. St. George, of Virginia. Paid $85.45 December 19, 1930.

Underhill, Charles L., of Massachusetts. Paid $125 February 2, 1931. Also, on the same date, paid $125 to cover accumulated credits for 1930. Total payment, $250.

Underwood, Mell G., of Ohio. Paid $125 January 30, 1931.

232

Vestal, Albert H., of Indiana. Paid $125 March 9, 1931.
so, on the same date, paid $106.18 to cover accumulated
dits for 1930. Total payment, $231.18.

Vinson, Carl, of Georgia. Paid $125 December 16, 1930.
so, February 25, 1931, paid $44.26 to cover accumulated
dits for 1930. Total payments, $169.26.

Wainwright, J. Mayhew, of New York. Paid $125 March
1931. Also, on the same date, paid $40.98 to cover accumu-
ed credits for 1930. Total payment, $165.98.

Walker, Lewis L., of Kentucky. Paid $122.60 January 21,
31.

Warren, Lindsay C., of North Carolina. Paid $96.56 Decem-
r 16, 1930.

Watres, Laurence H., of Pennsylvania. Paid $115.08 Feb-
ary 13, 1931.

Watson, Henry W., of Pennsylvania. Paid $125 December
1930.

Welsh, George A., of Pennsylvania. Paid $26.75 June 17,
31.

White, Wallace H., of Maine. Paid $125 March 6, 1931.
so, on the same date, paid $13.71 to cover accumulated
dits for 1929, and on November 5, 1930, paid $125 to cover
umulated credits for 1930. Total payments, $263.71.

Whitehead, Joseph, of Virginia. Paid $125 February 13,
31.

Whittington, M. W., of Mississippi. Paid $125 December
1931. Also, on the same date, paid $125 to cover accumu-
ed credits for 1930. Total payment, $250.

Wilson, Riley J., of Louisiana. Paid $125 December 20,
30.

Wright, William C., of Georgia. Paid $79.36 December 1930.

Zihlman, F. N., of Maryland. Paid $125 March 5, 19 Also, on the same date, paid $200.25 to cover accumulat credits for 1930 and 1929. Total payment, $325.25.

Appendix C

Nepotism

Twenty-six Senators and 97 Representatives have placed
the federal pay roll clerks of the same names as their
vn. These clerks draw pay for services in the offices of
eir patron members of Congress. In practically every
se, the clerk is a relative of the member. In addition, a
nsiderable number of members is reported to have
aced on the pay roll other persons connected with them
marriage.

From Senate Document No. 1, the list of such clerks
the pay roll for services in Senators' offices is obtained.
hat listing is as of June 30, 1931. The listing of clerks
ployed by Representatives was made public May 20,
32, by the Sergeant at Arms of the House in response
a resolution requiring such action. It gives the names
clerks employed at that time.

Following is the list of Senators and their clerks:

Senator Henry J. Ashurst of Arizona. The pay roll listed
izabeth R. Ashurst as assistant clerk to this Senator at $2,400
year.

Senator John H. Bankhead of Alabama. The pay roll listed
. W. Bankhead as clerk to this Senator at $3,900 a year.

Senator Alben B. Barkley of Kentucky. The pay roll lis
David M. Barkley as clerk to this Senator at $3,900 a ye
also L. L. Barkley as additional clerk at $1,800 a year.

Senator Hugo L. Black of Alabama. The pay roll lis
Josephine F. Black as assistant clerk to this Senator at $2,2
a year.

Senator Smith W. Brookhart of Iowa. The pay roll list
Florence H. Brookhart and Edith A. Brookhart as assista
clerks to this Senator at $2,220 a year, the latter replacing t
former on June 1, 1931.

Senator William J. Bulow of South Dakota. The pay r
listed William J. Bulow, Jr., as clerk to this Senator at $3,9
a year.

Senator Porter H. Dale of Vermont is Chairman of t
Committee on Civil Service. The pay roll listed Amy P. D.
as assistant clerk to the committee at $2,220 a year.

Senator Simeon D. Fess of Ohio is Chairman of the Co
mittee on the Library. The pay roll listed Dorothy Fess
assistant clerk to the committee at $2,220 a year.

Senator Lynn J. Frazier of North Dakota is Chairman
the Committee on Indian Affairs. The pay roll listed Vern
A. Frazier as additional clerk to the committee at $1,800
year.

Senator Walter F. George of Georgia. The pay roll list
Heard F. George as assistant clerk to this Senator at $2,400
year.

Senator Thomas P. Gore of Oklahoma. The pay roll list
Nina K. Gore as assistant clerk to this Senator at $2,220 a ye
a year.

Senator Pat Harrison of Mississippi. The pay roll list
Catherine Harrison as assistant clerk to this Senator at $2,4
a year.

Senator Felix Hebert of Rhode Island. The pay roll listed
Marguerite Hebert as additional clerk to this Senator at $1,800
year.

Senator William H. King of Utah. The pay roll listed Paul
King as assistant clerk to this Senator at $2,220 a year.

Senator Robert M. LaFollette of Wisconsin is Chairman of
Committee on Manufactures. The pay roll listed Rachel
Young LaFollette as assistant clerk to the committee at $2,400
year.

Senator M. M. Logan of Kentucky. The pay roll listed Ben
Logan as additional clerk to this Senator at $1,800 a year.

Senator Kenneth McKellar of Tennessee. The pay roll
listed D. W. McKellar as clerk to this Senator at $3,900 a year.

Senator Gerald P. Nye of North Dakota is Chairman of the
Committee on Public Lands and Surveys. The pay roll listed
Donald O. Nye as assistant clerk to the committee at $2,880 a
year.

Senator Roscoe C. Patterson of Missouri. The pay roll listed
H. Patterson as additional clerk to this Senator at $1,800 a
year.

Senator Thomas D. Schall of Minnesota is Chairman of the
Committee on Interoceanic Canals. The pay roll listed M. H.
Schall as clerk to the committee at $3,900 a year.

Senator Hubert D. Stephens of Mississippi. The pay roll
listed Hubert Stephens, Jr., as assistant clerk to this Senator
$2,400 a year.

Senator Elmer Thomas of Oklahoma. The pay roll listed
Edith Thomas as clerk to this Senator at $3,900 a year.

Senator Thomas G. Townsend of Delaware. The pay roll
listed Paul Townsend as his clerk at $3,900 a year. Senator

Townsend is a member of the Committee on Agriculture a
Forestry which employed Grace C. Townsend as assistant cl
at $2,400 a year.

Senator Park Trammell of Florida. The pay roll listed I
R. Trammell as assistant clerk to this Senator at $2,400 a ye
also Daisye L. Trammell as assistant clerk at $2,220 a year

Senator David I. Walsh of Massachusetts. The pay r
listed John W. Walsh as assistant clerk to this Senator
$2,400 a year.

Senator Burton K. Wheeler of Montana. The pay roll list
Elizabeth H. Wheeler as additional clerk to this Senator
$1,800 a year.

The list of Representatives follows, the name of t
Representative being given first, followed by the name
the clerk and the annual salary:

Abernethy, Charles L., of North Carolina. Clerk: Ma
N. Abernethy, $2,100.

Allen, John C., of Illinois. Clerk: John C. Allen, Jr., $1,4

Andresen, August H., of Minnesota. Clerk: Julia Andrese
$2,000.

Arentz, Samuel S., of Nevada. Clerk: Harriet K. Aren
$2,200.

Bankhead, William B., of Alabama. Clerk: Florence Ban
head, $2,000.

Barton, William E., of Missouri. Clerk: M. T. Barto
$2,500.

Blanton, Thomas L., of Texas. Clerk: Annie Louise Bla
ton, $3,000.

Bohn, Frank P., of Michigan. Clerk: Martena Bohn, $1,8

Boland, Patrick J., of Pennsylvania. Clerk: J. J. Boland,
500.

Brand, Charles, of Ohio. Clerk: Vance Brand, $3,080; and
therine Brand, $1,920.

Brumm, George F., of Pennsylvania. Clerk: Susan I.
umm, $2,300.

Burtness, Olger B., of North Dakota. Clerk: Z. E. Burtness,
500.

Busby, Jeff, of Mississippi. Clerk: J. M. Busby, $3,100.

Carter, Albert F., of California. Clerk: Martha L. Carter,
000.

Cartwright, Wilburn, of Oklahoma. Clerk: Carrie Cart-
ight, $2,100.

Cavicchia, Peter A., of New Jersey. Clerk: Priscilla J.
vicchia, $2,000.

Chindblom, Carl R., of Illinois. Clerk: Ruth C. Chind-
m, $125.

Chiperfield, Burnett M., of Illinois. Clerk: Robert B. Chip-
ield, $3,900.

Christgau, Victor, of Minnesota. Clerk: Milton Christgau,
000.

Clague, Frank, of Minnesota. Clerk: Stella Clague, $2,600.

Clark, J. Bayard, of North Carolina. Clerk: Martha Clark,
100.

Collier, James W., of Mississippi. Clerk: Laura D. Collier,
160.

Collins, Ross A., of Mississippi. Clerk: A. G. Collins,
900.

Colton, Don B., of Utah. Clerk: Mera Colton, $2,256.

Connery, William P., of Massachusetts. Clerk: L. J. C⟨
nery, $1,440.

Cooke, Edmund F., of New York. Clerk: Eileene J. Cool
$1,980.

Cooper, John G., of Ohio. Clerk: Manning D. Coop⟨
$1,800.

Crosser, Robert, of Ohio. Clerk: Barbara Crosser, $2,500

Crowther, Frank, of New York. Clerk: Peggy Y. Cro⟨
ther, $1,900.

Curry, Charles F., of California. Clerk: Florence A. Cur⟨
$2,360.

DeRouen, Rene L., of Louisiana. Clerk: Louis R. DeRou⟨
$3,000.

Dickinson, Clement C., of Missouri. Clerk: Peyton Dick⟨
son, $1,640.

Dominick, Fred H., of South Carolina. Clerk: Harry ⟨
Dominick, $1,100.

Englebright, Harry L., of California. Clerk: Grace Eng⟨
bright, $1,600.

Eslick, Edward E., of Tennessee. Clerk: Willa B. Eslic⟨
$3,200.

Feisinger, William L., of Ohio. Clerk: Lois Feising⟨
$2,000.

Fernandez, Joachim O., of Louisiana. Clerks: John ⟨
Fernandez, $3,800, and Viola M. Fernandez, $1,200.

Foss, Frank H., of Massachusetts. Clerk: Ruth H. Fo⟨
$1,200.

Freeman, Richard P., of Connecticut. Clerk: F. B. Fr⟨
man, $3,800.

Fuller, Claude A., of Arkansas. Clerk: May Fuller, $1,1⟨

Fulmer, Hampton P., of South Carolina. Clerk: Willa Fulmer, $3,200.

Garner, John N., of Texas. Clerk: Mrs. John N. Garner, $3,900.

Garrett, Daniel E., of Texas. Clerk: Ida O. Garrett, $2,600.

Gasque, Allard H., of South Carolina. Clerk: Bessie M. Gasque, $2,200.

Gillen, Courtland C., of Indiana. Clerk: Mary E. Gillen, $2,000.

Goodwin, Godfrey G., of Minnesota. Clerk: Alden N. Goodwin, $2,600.

Green, Robert A., of Florida. Clerk: W. H. Green, $3,500.

Greenwood, Arthur H., of Indiana. Clerk: Nettie B. Greenwood, $1,200.

Gregory, William V., of Kentucky. Clerk: Noble J. Gregory, $2,500.

Griffin, Anthony J., of New York. Clerk: Katherine L. Griffin, $2,000.

Hall, Thomas, of North Dakota. Clerk: Edna Hall, $3,300.

Hartley, Fred A., of New Jersey. Clerk: Henry A. Hartley, $1,400.

Hill, Samuel B., of Washington. Clerk: Barbara W. Hill, $2,100.

Holaday, William P., of Illinois. Clerk: Helen E. Holaday, $2,800.

Hooper, Joseph L., of Michigan. Clerk: Gertrude C. Hooper, $2,300.

Howard, Edgar, of Nebraska. Clerk: Elizabeth Howard, $1,100.

Johnson, Jed, of Oklahoma. Clerk: Beatrice Johnson, $2,500.

Kemp, Bolivar E., of Louisiana. Clerk: Lallie C. Kemp, $2,000.

Kvale, Paul J., of Minnesota. Clerk: Russell B. Kvale, $2,500.

Larrabee, William H., of Indiana. Clerk: Audrey M. Larrabee, $1,600.

Larsen, William W., of Georgia. Clerk: W. W. Larsen, Jr., $1,500.

Loofbourow, Frederick C., of Utah. Clerk: Huntington Loofbourow, $1,520.

Lozier, Ralph F., of Missouri. Clerk: Ralph Lozier, Jr., $3,600.

Maas, Melvin J., of Minnesota. Clerk: Gene Maas, $1,100.

Magrady, Frederick W., of Pennsylvania. Clerk: James Magrady, $2,200.

Manlove, Joe J., of Missouri. Clerk: Alma W. Manlove, $3,500.

Mansfield, Joseph J., of Texas. Clerk: Margaret Mansfield, $2,500.

May, Andrew J., of Kentucky. Clerk: Julia G. May, $3,000.

Montet, Numa F., of Louisiana. Clerk: Bonnie J. Montet $1,200.

Nelson, John E., of Maine. Clerk: Charles P. Nelson, $3,500.

Nelson, John M., of Wisconsin. Clerk: Grace L. Nelson, $2,500.

Parks, Tilman B., of Arkansas. Clerk: Jo Parks, $2,000.

Patterson, La Fayette L., of Alabama. Clerk: Nannie J. Patterson, $2,300.

Peavey, Hubert H., of Wisconsin. Clerk: Ella S. Peavey, $2,900.

Ragon, Heartsill, of Arkansas. Clerk: Mattie Ragon, $1,100.

Rainey, Henry T., of Illinois. Clerk: Ellen M. Rainey, $2,500.

Rankin, John E., of Mississippi. Clerk: A. L. Rankin, $2,600.

Romjue Milton A., of Missouri. Clerk: Lawson Romjue, $2,500.

Selvig, Conrad G., of Minnesota. Clerk: Helen M. Selvig, $2,900.

Schafer, John C., of Wisconsin. Clerk: Elsie W. Schafer, $3,700.

Shallenberger, Ashton C., of Nebraska. Clerk: Grace Shallenberger, $3,800.

Sinclair, James H., of North Dakota. Clerk: Daniel M. Sinclair, $1,100.

Sparks, Charles I., of Kansas. Clerk: Charles A. Sparks, $3,000.

Swank, Fletcher B., of Oklahoma. Clerk: Ada Swank, $2,500.

Tarver, Malcolm C., of Georgia. Clerk: M. C. Tarver, Jr., $2,000.

Taylor, Edward T., of Colorado. Clerk: Etta Taylor, $1,500.

Temple, Henry W., of Pennsylvania. Clerk: Edward L. Temple, $1,500.

Thatcher, Maurice H., of Kentucky. Clerks: F. H. Thatcher, $3,040, and A. B. Thatcher, $1,960.

Timberlake, Charles B., of Colorado. Clerk: Roberta E. Timberlake, $1,200.

Turpin, C. Murray, of Pennsylvania. Clerk: Margaret Turpin, $2,400.

Vinson, Carl, of Georgia. Clerk: Mary G. Vinson, $1,400.

Williams, Clyde, of Missouri. Clerk: Lola M. Williams, $2,600.

Williams, Guinn, of Texas. Clerks: M. Williams, $3,800, and Marie Williams, $1,200.

Wilson, Riley J., of Louisiana. Clerk: Riley J. Wilson, Jr., $3,900.

Wood, John S., of Georgia. Clerk: Jessie D. Wood, $2,500.

Wright, William C., of Georgia. Clerk: R. M. Wright, $2,200.

Yates, Richard, of Illinois. Clerk: Helen W. Yates, $3,000.

*   *   *   *   *

Osias, Camilo, Resident Commissioner, Philippine Islands. Clerk: Ildefonsa C. Osias, $2,500.

Wickersham, James, Delegate from Alaska. Clerk: Grace E. Wickersham, $1,100.

Appendix D

Select Committees of the Senate

The Select Committee to Investigate Contributions and Expenses of Senatorial Candidates (See Chapter VIII) was composed of the following Senators:

Chairman—Gerald P. Nye, of North Dakota.
Porter H. Dale, of Vermont.
Robert F. Wagner, of New York.
Clarence C. Dill, of Washington.
Roscoe C. Patterson, of Missouri.

The Special Committee on Conservation of Wild Life Resources (See Chapters III and IV) was composed of the following Senators:

Chairman—Frederic C. Walcott, of Connecticut.
Harry B. Hawes, of Missouri.
Key Pittman, of Nevada.
Charles L. McNary, of Oregon.
Peter Norbeck, of South Dakota.

The Special Select Committee to Investigate the Alaska Railroad (See Chapter VI) was composed of the following Senators:

Chairman—Robert B. Howell, of Nebraska.
John J. Kendrick, of Wyoming.
John Thomas, of Idaho.

The Select Committee on Post-Office Leases (See Chapter VI) was composed of the following Senators:

Chairman—John J. Blaine, of Wisconsin.
Daniel O. Hastings, of Delaware.
Felix Hebert, of Rhode Island.
Walter F. George, of Georgia.
Carl Hayden, of Arizona.

246

Appendix E

The Cost of Congress

To meet expenses of the House of Representatives, the Clerk of the House disbursed $3,780,615.39 during the fiscal year 1931. A small part of that amount was paid to meet bills incurred prior to 1931. In addition, there were paid salaries of 440 Representatives and Delegates at $10,000 a year apiece, and mileage of Representatives, for which $175,000 was appropriated.

Disbursements by the Secretary of the Senate during the fiscal year 1931 totaled $3,531,832.91. That figure included both salaries and mileage of Senators. A small part of the total, as in the case of the House, was to satisfy bills incurred prior to 1931.

The actual outlays of the two Houses during 1931 thus totaled $7,312,448.30. The approximate payments to cover salaries and mileage in the House were $4,575,000. The exact amount is not made public in the accounting, but the foregoing doubtless is within a few thousands of the actual disbursements. The death of several members during the year (terminating salaries in each case) and other factors cause the total to vary slightly from year to year. The two amounts, $7,312,448.30 actual outlays and $4,-

575,000 for House salaries and mileage, total $11,887,-448.30. That, within a few thousand dollars, is what it cost to maintain Congress in 1931.

Here are the detailed disbursements, as shown by House Document No. 2 and Senate Document No. 1:

House

Salaries of officers and employees	$1,008,590.41
Clerk hire, Members and Delegates	2,171,904.32
Stationery	92,674.97
Folding documents	16,087.25
Materials for folding	2,145.36
Furniture and repairs	35,628.76
Miscellaneous items (supplies, etc.)	77,432.52
Stenographic reports of Committee hearings	17,059.16
Expenses of Special and Select Committees	112,381.68
Telegraph and telephone service	127,980.10
Speaker's automobile	5,363.86
Salaries, Capitol Police	43,726.50
Contingent fund, Capitol Police	100.00
Joint Committee on Printing	5,575.00
Legislative Counsel (preparing bills, etc.)	31,974.20
Packing boxes	6,814.68
Special Services compiling documents	5,000.00
Payments for contesting seats in Congress	15,778.23
Postage	1,150.00
Attending physician (supplies)	748.39
Portrait of Nicholas Longworth	2,500.00
Total	$3,780,615.39

APPENDIX

Senate

Salaries of Senators	$ 954,863.05
Mileage of Senators	46,627.20
Salary of the Vice-President	15,000.00
Salaries of officers and employees	1,608,493.19
Salaries of Capitol Police	43,704.00
Contingent fund, Capitol Police	100.00
Uniforms and equipment, Capitol Police	3,375.00
Automobile and maintenance, Vice-President	7,720.36
Legislative Counsel (preparing bills, etc.)	25,380.35
Reporting debates (official stenographers)	60,340.00
Salaries and expenses, Joint Committee on Printing	5,810.00
Cleaning furniture	3,746.64
Repairs of furniture	2,700.35
Purchase of furniture	5,490.88
Expenses of inquiries and investigations	424,408.04
Folding documents	11,149.00
Materials for folding	1,983.94
Fuel for heating apparatus	1,683.65
Kitchens and restaurants	52,171.47
Mail transportation	12,905.58
Miscellaneous items (supplies, etc.)	184,814.26
Packing boxes	938.04
Postage	350.00
Stationery	33,877.91
Storage of documents	2,000.00
Payments for extra services	2,200.00
Payments to widows of Senators (two at $10,000)	20,000.00
Total	$3,531,832.91

THE END